Contents

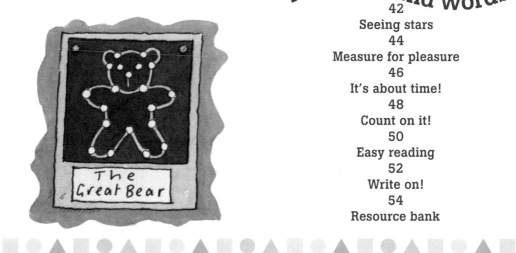

The Great Bear

Contents

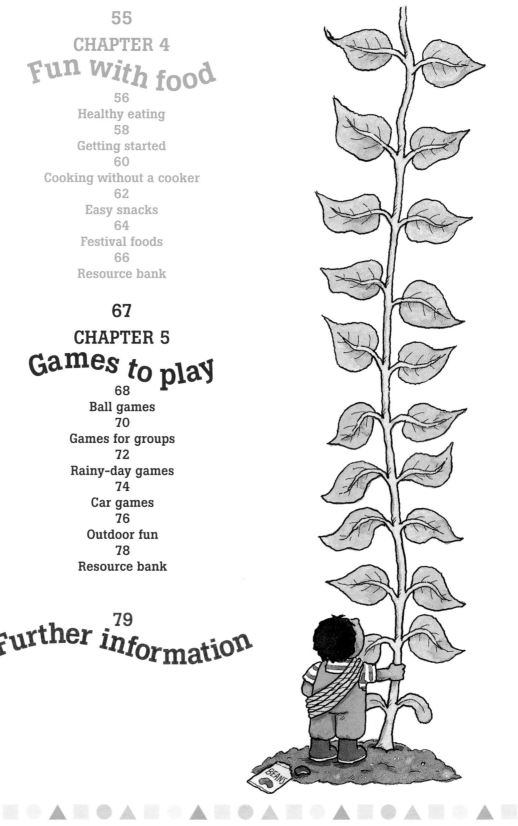

OR AGES
0–8

Cre   play

INDOOR AND
OUTDOOR FUN

INSTANT IDEAS!

ACTI

Produced on behalf of the
National Childminding
Association

ncma

SCHOLASTIC

ALISON COLEMAN

BK43775

Credits

British Library Cataloguing-in-Publication Data
A catalogue record for this book is available from the British Library.

ISBN 0 439 98498 X

The right of Alison Coleman to be identified as the author of this work has been asserted by her in accordance with the Copyright, Designs and Patents Act 1988.

Author
Alison Coleman

Editor
Sally Gray

Assistant Editor
Kate Element

Series Designer
Lynne Joesbury

Designer
Catherine Mason

Illustrations
Jessica Stockham/Beehive Illustration

Text © 2003 Alison Coleman
© 2003 Scholastic Ltd

Designed using Adobe PageMaker

Published by Scholastic Ltd
Villiers House
Clarendon Avenue
Leamington Spa
Warwickshire CV32 5PR

Visit our website at www.scholastic.co.uk

Printed by Belmont Press

3 4 5 6 7 8 9 0   5 6 7 8 9 0 1 2

Acknowledgements

Some of the material in this book has been previously published in *Who Minds?*, NCMA's membership magazine.

Every effort has been made to trace copyright holders and the publishers apologise for any inadvertent omissions.

Introduction

What is NCMA?

The National Childminding Association (NCMA) is the only national charity and membership organisation that speaks on behalf of registered childminders in England and Wales. The organisation promotes quality registered childminding so that children, families and communities can benefit from the best in childcare and education. NCMA has a thriving membership of registered childminders, parents and local authorities who enjoy a range of benefits, including a members' handbook, a quarterly magazine, *Who Minds?,* free legal advice and legal representation, plus a range of services and insurance products specially tailored to the needs of registered childminders.

All NCMA childminders are expected to work towards ten Quality Standards. These cover all aspects of childminding, including safety, nutrition, managing children's behaviour, equal opportunities, and good business practice. The Quality Standards state that NCMA childminders must never use physical punishment and must make sure that children are cared for in a smoke-free environment.

For more information about NCMA, visit their website at www.ncma.org.uk

Why *Creative Play*?

To celebrate 25 years of NCMA, Scholastic has joined with NCMA to make a collection of the play ideas that have been featured in *Who Minds?*, in an updated and revised format, along with some exciting new ideas. This collection will provide plenty of inspiration for parents and childminders alike, and is ideal for anyone who looks after children under the age of eight, especially if they are responsible for children of different

Introduction

ages at the same time. There are creative ideas for indoor and outdoor play, music, crafts, make-believe play and art projects – all using everyday materials and equipment.

Learning through play

The fact that children like to play is something we perhaps take for granted, yet play is fundamental to the development of some of their most important life skills – how to share, how to be a team player, how to make friends and how to interact socially with peers and adults. By taking an active role in children's early play development, you will encourage their creativity, self-expression, and enquiring minds.

Play is important in the development of a number of key skill areas, one of the most important being children's educational development. It has been suggested that children who are encouraged to express themselves freely through play are more able to adapt and learn new skills and perform

better at school. Play that has been planned and carefully structured will certainly encourage them to explore, ask questions and try something new. It can help children approach the exciting challenges of school with a positive frame of mind. By playing word and number games for fun during the pre-school years, children may find the transition to the more complex numeracy and literacy tasks they face at school a little easier. Introducing them to a wide range of craft materials and resources will help them to use their imagination to the full during art and craft activities. An early introduction to food, where it comes from and how it is made, can help to set healthy, sensible eating habits for life.

Play is good for children's health and well-being. For several years, child health experts have expressed fears that children who lead sedentary lives may be storing up health problems for the future. While television, the Internet and the new technologies have revolutionised children's lives and the way they find out about their world, it is important that they do not hold a monopoly over them. Outdoor activities such as organised sports, special days out, or even an hour or two in the garden, will help to keep growing children fit and healthy. Even on the wettest day there is no excuse for becoming a 'couch potato' – indoor games are just as much fun. Physical activities build stamina, improve physical co-ordination and maintain an active mind and body.

Play is vital for emotional development. Where better to explore your own and other people's feelings than through interactive play? How do the children feel when someone is not playing by the rules, or does not want to share? How do other people feel when you do the same? And how good does it feel to achieve something as part of a team – even if it is only third place in the egg and spoon race! Young children can find it quite difficult to understand the impact of their behaviour on others, but by playing and interacting with other children, they will learn to find out.

Exploring cultures and communities

Play is the natural way to explore other cultures and communities – the world that exists beyond the immediate circle of friends and family. This is one of the most important concepts that children need to learn about – and here, creative play comes into its own. Initially children should have a clear understanding of their own culture and community, as defined by their immediate and extended family and social circle. This will help them to develop a sense of belonging and provide them with a strong self-image.

Role-play provides valuable opportunities for children to explore their own cultures and helps them to appreciate the similarities and differences in others. It then becomes an easy step to introduce the children to a wide range of different cultures and religions, through activities such as storytelling, cultural cookery, listening to music, dressing-up in costumes that represent different cultures and using resources that reflect these – such as clothes, cooking implements, vegetables, badges, symbols, candles and toys. This play will strengthen children's awareness of the cultures and customs of others.

As children begin to learn about their own and other people's worlds, they can be taken to visit cultural centres and introduced to people from different cultures within the community, many of whom will be delighted to talk to young children about the origins and day-to-day reality of their culture. In making cultural and community exploration an enjoyable part of play, children will naturally become more aware of, and more sensitive, to the needs and feelings of others and learn to respect other people's cultures and beliefs.

How to use this book

As well as a comprehensive introduction, planning section and further information sections, this book is divided into five main chapters, covering different areas of play. The chapters are: 'Out and about'; 'Arts and

crafts'; 'Numbers and words'; 'Fun with food' and 'Games to play'.

The activity ideas are concise and imaginative – some are short and can be done when there is less time available, others are indoor activities for wet days, and there are many other ideas, including mind games, to break up the most monotonous car journey. You can mix and match activities from several different chapters to help you organise a varied and stimulating play activity schedule for a day, a week or even several weeks in advance. A seasonal planner (pages 9 and 10) will help you to look even further ahead and arrange special activities that are relevant to key dates and events throughout the year.

Adapting ideas to suit different age ranges

The activities in this book are suitable for a wide range of ages and include suggestions for babies and young toddlers and from three-year-olds who are exploring the kitchen for the first time, to older children who can produce wonderfully simple dishes with minimum assistance. The key lies in planning activities carefully, understanding what the various age groups are capable of managing, and deciding on the appropriate resources and equipment to use. Safety issues are

addressed throughout the book. It is important that even the youngest children are made aware of safety issues, and where appropriate, children should be made responsible for helping to implement safety procedures for themselves.

This book and the Foundation Stage and National Curriculum

Creative play that is encouraged from an early age can help to prepare children for the Foundation Stage (ages 3 to 5) and Key Stage 1 (ages 5 to 7) of the National Curriculum. The Foundation Stage (see *Curriculum Guidance for the Foundation Stage*, published by QCA publications, www.qca.org.uk) is important in preparing children for later schooling. Children are helped to master 'Stepping Stones' along the way to achieving 'Early Learning Goals' in six 'Areas of Learning' – Personal, social and emotional development; Communication, language and literacy; Mathematical development; Knowledge and understanding of the world; Physical development; and Creative development, laying a secure basis for Key Stage 1 and beyond. Personal, social and health education, and citizenship, although not compulsory at Key Stage 1, are being encouraged. The activities in this book can be used equally well within the guidelines for early years in Scotland, Northern Ireland and Wales.

The wide range of activities in this book will help to put young children on the right track, or may support older children's learning at school. By completing these activities you will be helping children to make connections between different areas of learning and to gain a better understanding of the world around them.

Equal opportunities

Inclusion is an important issue. Regardless of social and cultural background, or any disabilities they may have, children need to feel that they belong to a group and have the same opportunities to achieve as everyone else. This book encompasses multicultural elements, such as food, festivals, outings and traditions, with the aim of encouraging children to be interested in, and accepting of, the wider community. For children with disabilities, some of the activities may need a little extra care in planning, and useful contacts for help and information on special resources or equipment are included in the 'Further information' section at the end of the book (pages 79–80).

Working with parents and the community

Creative play activities that are carefully structured can help children to learn some of the important life skills they need for a happy, independent life. The activities should also help them to show consideration for the needs and feelings of others. The benefits of play do not have to end with the game, or the junk modelling session; they should extend to their everyday life at home, at school, and when they are out and about. They can easily be facilitated by communicating with parents and other members of the community in order to establish a continuity of play development. It is also important to remember that your work is in partnership with the children's parents and that communication between you is vital in order to ensure the maximum benefits of your care and work with the children.

Play is not just for fun – it is for life. In using this book we hope you have as much fun playing the activities as we have had compiling them!

Planning

Most of the creative play ideas in this book are suitable for doing, weather permitting, at any time of the year, but it is a good idea to have some activities planned to coincide with special occasions. Highlight key holidays and festival days on a bright wall calendar and add some of the more unusual cultural festival dates, such as some of the ones listed on these pages.

Planning

With so many creative play ideas to try, the biggest problem might be knowing where to start! But the key to productive and enjoyable creative play lies in the planning. You need to think about how much time you have available for any one activity and to make sure that all the materials you will need are available.

One step at a time

Do not have too many ideas on the go at once. Think about the children's ages and what realistically they are capable of achieving. They will tire of activities that are so difficult that you have to intervene and do most of it for them. Young children have limited attention spans – around 15 to 20 minutes is the optimum time span for concentration. Plan with this in mind, keeping your schedule a mixture of short and manageable activities. When you are planning number and word activities try to choose a quiet time of the day when there are less likely to be distractions and the children can concentrate.

Thinking ahead

Things like weather and available time will determine some of the activities, but do not forget to allow some extra time for setting up materials and clearing away afterwards, or for travelling if you are going outdoors. Plan more ambitious projects well in advance. Group games and some of the outdoor play activities are more fun if you can get larger numbers of children to take part. Encourage your childminding group to meet for outdoor sessions, or even invite friends, neighbours and family along for a fun activity day, but plan well in advance and have wet-weather contingencies!

If you are making models or working on craft projects that must be left to dry, make sure that you have somewhere safe to leave them where they will not cause a mess or get damaged.

Any activities that involve food need extra careful planning. If you have room in your kitchen cupboards, set aside a small space where the children can store some of their basic tinned and dry ingredients. They will enjoy taking some of the responsibility for planning by ensuring that there are enough ingredients for cooking days, and letting you know when it is time to buy some more.

Seasonal activity planner
Spring
Festivals
- St David's Day (1 March)
- St Patrick's Day (17 March)
- Holi (March/April)
- Mother's Day (March/April)
- Easter (March/April)
- Pesach/Passover (March/April)
- April Fool's Day (1 April)
- Baisakhi (14 April)
- St George's Day (23 April)
- May Day (1 May)
- Kodomono-hi/Japanese Children's Day (5 May)

Spring activity links
- 'In the garden', pages 12–13
- 'Come rain or shine', pages 18–19

> **Notes**
> By March/April, activities can be focused around the Easter festival – daffodils, spring lambs and Easter chicks provide excellent themes for craft and play ideas.

Planning

Summer

Festivals
- Shavuot (May/June)
- Wesak (May/June)
- Midsummer's Day (24 June)
- Father's Day (June)
- Dragon Boat Festival (June)
- St Swithun's Day (15 July)
- Raksha Bandhan (July/August)
- O'bon (July/August)

Summer activity links
- 'Summer days out', pages 14–15
- 'Come rain or shine', pages 18–19
- 'Outdoor fun', pages 76–77

Notes
At this time of year, the weather will be warmer and sunnier, so you should be making the most of it, carrying out plenty of outdoor activities and going on visits to interesting places, such as gardens and parks. You can organise outdoor craft activities with the children – water games are especially welcome when it is hot – but avoid going outside around midday and make sure that you and the children put on plenty of suncream.

Autumn

Festivals
- Ethiopian New Year (11 September)
- Grandparent's Day (September)
- Chinese Moon Festival (September)
- Sukkot (September/October)
- Harvest Festival (September/October)
- Divali (October/November)
- Bonfire Night (5 November)
- St Andrew's Day (30 November)
- Guru Nanak's birthday (November)

Autumn activity links
- 'Festival foods', pages 64–65
- 'Rainy-day games', pages 72–73

Notes
In autumn, nature provides some of the most colourful and interesting craft materials, so go out on walks in your local area and help the children to collect natural items such as fallen autumn leaves, acorns and horse chestnuts. You can also make up some simple home-made food baskets for the Harvest Festival, traditionally distributed around the parish by the local church.

Winter

Festivals
- Hanukkah (November/December)
- Christmas Day (25 December)
- Eid-ul-Fitr (December/January)
- New Year's Day (1 January)
- Epiphany (6 January)
- Chinese New Year (January/February)
- Candlemas (2 February)
- Valentine's Day (14 February)
- Mardi Gras/Shrove Tuesday (February/March)

Winter activity links
- 'Come rain or shine', pages 18–19
- 'Festival foods', pages 64–65

Notes
As Christmas approaches, the children will enjoy making decorations and cards, reading the Christmas story and planning favourite Christmas party games. Chinese New Year in January or February, coming so soon after the 1 January celebrations, is an opportunity to look at why different cultures have different calendars and how they celebrate the start of a new year.

For festival activities, see the *Around the Year* series (Scholastic).

CHAPTER 1

Out and about

Whether at the seaside, in a busy town or simply enjoying time in the garden, children adore outside experiences and they can be a lot of fun. This chapter will help you to think of new ways to entertain and challenge your children as you take them out and about.

Why 'out and about'?

Children learn best when they are motivated and when the learning is made fun for them. Activities that are relevant to children's interests, and experiences that are new and exciting are two ways to motivate and enthuse young children. And apart from anything else, it is often easier to go outdoors to play when the children have got excess energy!

Young children have an eager interest and enthusiasm for activities that take place outdoors. From a young age, most children are naturally curious and want to find out about the world around them. Your role, of course, is not only to show them these things, but to enrich their experiences while making them safe. The ideas in this chapter will show you how.

A range of ages

Children of varying ages will experience the outdoor world differently. A young baby will be interested in light and shadow, gurgling happily on a blanket whilst looking at the shapes and movement of a tree blowing in the wind; toddlers will want to dig and explore, chase and investigate; and older children will make more considered observations of the things that they find and notice. The activity suggestions in this chapter will provide helpful suggestions.

Special advice

Safety issues are obviously of paramount importance when taking young children into the outside world. Helpful tips and safety notes will be given throughout.

In the garden

Gardening is good fun. Whether it is indoors or out, small children derive great pleasure from planting their own seeds, caring for them and watching them grow into something pretty to look at – or something good to eat.

Caring for plants helps children to develop a sense of responsibility. The following activities provide lots of suggestions for growing, planting, eating and learning.

Children of different ages

▲ Toddlers will enjoy any kind of watering activity, and will enjoy 'helping' to dig over any prospective vegetable patches!

▲ Older children will enjoy making labels for the plants and can be encouraged to keep a growing plant diary charting the progress of their garden nursery empire!

Indoor gardening

Most of us will remember the joy of planting our first cress seeds, and then harvesting the results for a sandwich a few days later! This kind of instant success is a winner with very young children who are often not the most patient of creatures!

What to do

● Save the tops from root vegetables, such as carrots, swedes and parsnips. Place them cut side down on a piece of moistened kitchen towel in a shallow dish of water. Keep them warm and moist, and in a few days green shoots will appear from the top of the vegetable, then sprout into small plants.

■●▲■●▲■●▲■●▲■●▲■●▲■●▲■●▲■●▲■

● Grow runner bean seeds in jam jars. Place a piece of blotting paper around the inside of a jar, so that the bottom end is in contact with the base of the jar. Position the seed between the side of the jar and the paper. Keep the paper moist and watch the bean sprout grow – usually very quickly!

● Plant some vegetable seeds in growbags on a window sill in your home. Add lolly stick labels and water lovingly (following the instructions on the packet)! When the conditions are right, plant the children's nurtured seedlings in an appropriate patch in your garden.

Vegetables and herbs

Children are always delighted when they can eat the results of their work. These fun vegetable- and herb-planting ideas will get mouths watering!

What to do

● To grow herbs you will need a small pot, about 12cm deep, some multi-purpose compost and herb seeds (such as oregano, thyme, mint or rosemary). Fill the pot with compost and sprinkle the seeds thinly over the surface. Then sprinkle a layer of

compost, about 1mm deep over the seeds. Keep the seeds warm and moist. As the weather becomes milder, transfer the plants outdoors and create a herb garden with the children's help.

● To grow vegetables from seed you will need some small pots, compost, and thin garden stakes. Plant the seeds individually about 2cm deep in small pots. Keep the compost moist, but not too wet. Once the seedlings have grown accustom them gradually to the outdoors and plant out from May onwards. Support the plants with a frame of stakes.

Fun with flowers

Growing colourful flowers is a joy that hopefully the children will continue to experience throughout their lives. We can start them off in the following simple but significant ways.

What to do

● Sunflowers are always popular with children. The plants grow quickly and can be measured regularly. To grow sunflowers you will need some fairly deep containers, compost and garden stakes. Fill a container with compost and push a single seed into it.

● Water it lightly and leave to germinate in a warm place. Once established, plant the sunflower outside (watch out for slugs!). As it grows taller and thicker, support the stem with stakes.

● When your sunflowers have died at the end of the summer, cut off the heads and store them in a warm place until completely dry. You can then harvest the seeds and store them in an airtight container ready for planting next year. This is a good way of illustrating life-cycles for older children.

● Other flowers to try include nasturtiums, marigolds and pansies.

Safety matters

▲ Supervise all garden activities and keep all adult garden tools and equipment safely out of the children's reach.

▲ Garden sheds should be locked, with any dangerous, sharp or poisonous objects or substances kept well out of reach.

▲ If you have pets, make sure that you clean up after them.

▲ Teach children NEVER to eat seeds or berries that they find in the garden and ensure that they always wash their hands thoroughly after gardening.

▲ Invest in an information book about plants in order to find out about any poisonous plants that might be lurking in your garden.

Top tips

▲ There are garden tools made especially for little hands, but most young children are happy to use an old kitchen spoon or fork, and older ones can use adult trowels and forks (under supervision).

▲ If you can spare the space, allocate a patch of your garden for the children to cultivate. They will benefit from the sense of ownership and pride that they will get from maintaining their own little area.

▲ At first, try a quick-growing plant such as the runner bean for fast and tasty results!

CHAPTER
1
Out and about

Summer days out

Summer's here – time to pack away the indoor games and head for the open air! Better still, why not treat the children and make a day of it? Youngsters love the excitement of a special day out. Where you decide to go will depend on where you live and transport, but whether you choose the beach or the town, there are plenty of ways you can make it a day to remember.

Children of different ages

▲ Prepare some simple activity sheets or checklists for older children to use while on their outing.
▲ Use the opportunity to develop toddlers' vocabulary, whether it is animal names, seaside words such as sand and sea or town words such as bus, lorry and shop.

By the seaside

Even if you live near the sea, a visit to the seaside is a source of fun and excitement for everybody. Both sandy and pebbly beaches can provide some great games to enjoy!

When you're there

● Collect some shells and pebbles and use them to make pictures, or letters that spell out your names in the sand.
● Mark out an area of sand and bury some 'treasure' (such as a small coloured ball or beanbag) for the children to dig for.
● Build a miniature town of sandcastles with empty yoghurt pots left over from lunch.

At the farm

A visit to a farm can be a wonderful experience for children. They can see animals at close quarters, find out about where their food comes from and see exciting and unusual vehicles such as tractors, diggers and combine harvesters!

Safety matters

▲ Be extra careful around water.
▲ Ensure that the children do not pick any flowers, berries or seeds.
▲ Do not forget sun cream and sun-hats, and do not stay in the sun for too long.
▲ Take a small first-aid kit and make sure that you are aware of any allergies that the children have.
▲ Ensure that any farms you visit are clean and well managed and have washing facilities for the children to use before eating and coming home. Do not eat food near the animals.
▲ Only visit beaches that have been designated as safe and clean.

When you're there
● Find out as much as possible about the jobs that all the animals do on the farm, from providing milk to rounding up sheep.
● Look at the different types of farm machinery and discuss what they are used for. Look at the size of the wheels and any tools. What are the tools used for?
● Time your visit so that you can see some work in action, whether it is feeding the animals, shearing or milking.

At the park
Turn a visit to the park into a special occasion by going with a group of others. Try to pick a day after it has been dry for some time and take blankets to sit on.

When you're there
● Collect handfuls of natural objects such as twigs, leaves and pine cones for young children to sort and explore.
● Use twigs to lay a trail of arrows for the children to follow.
● Organise some egg and spoon and three-legged races.

Around the town
Older children might groan at the idea of a trip into town. Try boosting their interest by looking at buildings in a new way or introducing some fun games.

When you're there
● Take a 'heads and tails' walk. At every street corner, toss a coin and if it is heads, take a left turn, if it is tails, take a right. See where it takes you! Mark your route on a map with older children.
● Ask the children to try and tell which are old and which are new buildings.
● Make a note of all the different vehicles that you spot together.

In the country
Why not organise a nature walk and picnic in your nearby countryside? Your local library should be able to provide information on what to look out for.

When you're there
● Take crayons and paper and do some bark rubbings of different types of tree.
● See how many different types of bird you can hear or see. Help older children to use a bird guide to identify them.

Top tips
▲ Know the limits of your children – how good are they on long journeys?
▲ Share the day with others, as extra pairs of hands are very useful!
▲ Pack extra sets of clothes for any outing.
▲ Do not forget your camera!
▲ Check the weather forecast and tide timetables and be prepared for all eventualities.
▲ Sit below the tideline on a beach, so that you know that the sand has been regularly washed by the sea.

On the move

From a very early age, children are fascinated by things that go. Some of their first words are often car, bus, plane or tractor! Activities that involve looking at or making vehicles are always a big hit with children of all ages. Below are a few exciting suggestions!

Children of different ages

▲ Invite younger children to help you sort out the toy box, looking for vehicles of any kind. Refine the search by sorting the vehicles into different groups, such as those with wheels, or those that can fly and so on.
▲ Borrow some non-fiction books about vehicles from the library to share with older children. Read them first, so that you can answer their many questions!

horse-drawn

By land

The invention of the wheel revolutionised the way we live. From horse and carts to the motor car, people found new and more effective ways to go from place to place.

What to do

● Look at a selection of the children's toys. Which ones have wheels? Push them along and watch them go. What would happen if they had no wheels to move them along?

● Make some observation charts listing car colours such as red, green, blue and so on. Watch out of a window, or take a local walk to spot cars. Ask the children to mark down the colours of the cars that they see. After a set period of time, add up how many there are of each colour.
● Design some model cars using empty boxes. Push two skewers through the box and cut off the sharp ends. Add lumps of Plasticine to make wheels to ensure that the car moves. Once you have the basic body

Further ideas
▲ Place a heavy object, such as a big book on the table. Ask the children to push it from one end to the other. Now, place a row of about 20 pencils, side by side on the table and lie the book on top. Let the children feel how easily it now moves along the rollers.
▲ Take a trip on a steam railway or look at pictures of steam trains to find out what it was like to travel by train more than a century ago.
▲ Demonstrate, in simple terms, how an aeroplane flies by flying a kite. The string pulls the kite forward (like the thrust of the aeroplane engine) and the wind pushes it upwards, or gives it lift (like the air underneath the aeroplane wings).

■●▲■●▲■●▲■●▲■●▲■●▲■●▲■●▲

and wheels the children can add shiny or sticky paper to create their own style.

By sea

Travelling by ship or boat is generally a more leisurely form of transport. As well as being vehicles for people to travel on, boats are important for transporting goods and cargo. Look at a globe to notice how much of our planet is ocean – this gives us an idea of how vital sea travel is.

What to do

● Make simple yachts using pencils, pieces of balsa wood, Plasticine and paper sails. Push a pencil through some paper, close to one end, and then back out again close to the other end to make the sail. Stick a lump of Plasticine to the front of your piece of Balsa wood and push the pointed end of the pencil, now threaded through the sail, firmly into it to make your sailing-yacht!

● On a fine day fill a washing up bowl with water and take it into the garden with the boats. Hold a yacht race by blowing the boats with a straw.

By air

If you want to travel further and faster, an aeroplane can take you to the other side of the world in a day. Aeroplanes are a source of real fascination for children. If you live close enough, a trip to the airport makes a fascinating day out.

What to do

● Children of all ages love to fly paper aeroplanes, and there are plenty of papercraft books to borrow from the library showing unusual designs that fly amazingly well.

● Make some simple paper aeroplanes and decorate them with pencils and crayons. Have a competition to see whose plane can fly the furthest.

● Find out what other forms of air transport the children can think of, such as helicopters and hot air balloons.

● Do not forget travel to outer space and have some fun role-playing an exciting rocket trip to the stars!

Top tips

▲ Read some background information about the mechanics behind the most popular moving vehicles. Older children are bound to have endless questions about how things happen!

▲ Sort out a box of small world vehicles for the children to explore.

▲ Have a transport day out in the garden, with wheeled toys and giant recyclable models of cars and boats.

Come rain or shine

We have one of the most changeable climates in the world, so it is little wonder that we spend so much time thinking about the weather. Weather is a fascinating subject for children, especially if they have the chance to carry out some weather experiments of their own.

Children of different ages

▲ Whether adult, child or tiny baby we can all respond to the weather in some way. Babies and toddlers will marvel at the noise and movement of the wind and rain and will love the feel of the sun's warmth on their bodies as they play outside.

▲ Older children will ask more questions about why we get certain types of weather, and it is a good idea to have some basic information to hand in order to answer difficult questions!

Answering questions

▲ *How is snow made?* If the air temperature falls below freezing, the water vapour in the clouds can turn into ice particles, which fall as hail or snow instead of rain.

▲ *Why is it cold in winter?* Show the children a picture or model of our solar system, in particular the way that the Earth tilts on its axis so that different parts of the world are closer to the Sun at different times of the year. During winter we are tilted away from the Sun and the weather is much colder.

Sunshine

What better for a day out and about than some sunny weather to enjoy? But do not forget that the children will need sun protection, even when it is overcast.

What to do

● Go outside on a sunny day and stand in the warm path of the sun for a few moments. Talk about how it feels. Now stand in the shade. Talk about the difference together.

● How do we know hot air rises? Try blowing soap bubbles close to a warm radiator. The air that is warmed immediately above the radiator travels upwards, taking the bubbles with it!

Windy weather

It seems that windy weather is capable of getting children really excited! Try to harness some of that positive energy with these exhilarating ideas!

What to do

● Tie a long length of ribbon to the children's wrists and go outside on a windy day. Hold out your arms in the breeze and watch the ribbon fall and flutter as gusts of wind approach and recede.
● Go on a kite-flying outing. Find a suitable hill to run up and down and check out how strong the wind is, based on how well your kite flies! Younger children will simply enjoy the thrill of running up and down a hill in the wind!
● Look out for weather vanes on people's houses or farm buildings if you live in the countryside. Explain that from them you can tell in which direction the wind is blowing.

Rainy weather

Rainy weather is often responsible for spoiling our fun! But with a healthy splash of imagination and these fun ideas we can turn it to our advantage.

What to do

● Invest in some cheap waterproof trousers to slip on over boots. Go for a puddle-splashing walk together. Compare the sizes of the different puddles and let older children use plastic rulers to find out which are the deepest!
● Make some simple rain gauges to find out how much rain falls over a chosen period of time. Take an old plastic bottle and cut it in half. On the bottom half, measure out and, using a black waterproof marker pen, mark a scale in millimetres or centimetres,

depending on the length of time for which you are going to collect the rainwater. Turn the top half of the bottle upside down and put it into the bottom half of the bottle. This will act as a funnel to collect the rain. Every day or week, the children should take a reading of how much water is in the gauge and record it on a chart, before emptying the bottle and starting again.

Hail or snow

Most children need little encouragement to get their warm clothes on for an expedition in the snow! Aside from the endlessly popular pastimes of making snowmen and snowballs there are plenty of other ways to get the most from snow!

What to do

● Put on your cold-weather gear and arm yourselves with a magnifying glass. Look at a snowflake as it falls on a piece of dark material such as a coat. Notice the patterns and how each snowflake has six points.
● Make small snow sculptures. Choose a theme, such as shapes or furniture and use hands or small tools such as spoons, blunt knives and empty pots to create some wonderful designs.

Top tips

▲ Keep spare sun-hats, wellies, waterproofs and umbrellas so that you are equipped for all kinds of weather.
▲ Get some weather books out from your library. Some will have suggestions for making your own kites and more sophisticated weather stations.
▲ Watch the weather forecast with the children and talk about the symbols and expressions that the presenters use.

No place like home

Home means a lot of different things to us. It is the place of warmth, comfort and security. It is often full of colour, pattern and interesting things, and of course, structurally, it is made from a variety of materials and textures. The activities below provide some inspiring ways of looking at homes with the children.

Children of different ages

▲ Young children and toddlers love to play with small-world houses, people and furniture and can be encouraged to invent uses for small boxes and other recyclable materials.

▲ Encourage older children to work on longer-term projects, such as gradually building a house, room by room, from recyclable and collage materials. Ensure that you have a safe storage place for it during construction.

Constructing homes

It is unlikely that most children will ever have wondered what their home is made from, or how it was built. The ideas below will inspire them to take a closer look.

What to do

● The easiest way for children to understand how houses are built is to see it for themselves! It is likely that new houses are being built somewhere reasonably close to you. Take the children to watch the process from a safe distance. They will be enthralled by the foundation diggers, the bricklaying, timber work and roofing. If you make a

return visit at a later date you can see how quickly things have changed.

● Provide a construction kit such as LEGO or MEGA BLOKS and let the children experiment with building a new home. Provide toy diggers and trucks and encourage some imaginative play.

Further ideas

▲ Take some rubbings of the brick patterns of different types of building.

▲ On a fine day, set up a play tent in the garden. As well as being a fun place to play, it has the added bonus of providing protection from the sun!

● Look at the bricks that your own home is made from. Look at how they have been laid. Do they overlap? Back inside, experiment with different types of bricklaying using LEGO bricks (or similar). Which patterns make the strongest designs?

● Mix a little water with sand so that it is firm enough to make some sand brick structures in your sand tray or sandpit.

Homes all around us

Houses and homes are built in many different styles and from many different materials. Take a look in your local area to see the variety around you. Look out for materials particular to your locality.

What to do

● Take a drive in the car, or go for a walk and encourage the children to look at the different types of home they can see, from bungalow to narrowboat.

● Go for a walk to look for all the different types of material used for homes in your area. Look out for thatched, tiled or felt roofs; wood, glass, concrete, stone and brick walls.

● Rearrange a few chairs (or use a table) and drape sheets or blankets over them to make an indoor tent. Hold a tea-party inside it!

Homes around the world

All over the world, people use different materials to build their homes, depending on the climate and the materials available.

What to do

● Look at some non-fiction books that show homes in different parts of the world. Talk about which are the hot and which are the cold places. What materials have the people used? What design features help to keep their homes warm or cool?

● Make mini wigwams with the children. Provide each child with three twigs and a piece of circular material or paper. Cut a slit

in the material, one radius width, fold it into a cone shape and cut out an inner circle so that it fits around the top of the twigs. Stand up the twigs, with their base making a triangle, and tie the tops together. Fold the material cone in place over the twigs and fix with some more sticky tape.

Interiors

Inspire the children to make some colourful interior designs of their own with these ideas.

What to do

● Let the children make a box model of their own bedroom, perhaps with a new design or colour scheme. You will need plenty of cardboard boxes, as well as paints, material scraps and fixing materials. Use scraps of coloured material or paper for carpets and curtains. Items such as empty cotton reels can double up as tables.

● Provide the children with cheap plastic seed trays and go outside to make a miniature garden to go with the children's model homes. Fill the tray with a little soil, perhaps a dish of water for a pond and some pebbles for a rockery!

Just the job

'What do you want to be when you grow up?' is a question that is repeatedly asked of children. Many have interesting answers, some change their minds frequently. But, one thing is sure, the world of work is of endless fascination for children of all ages and they take delight in role-playing work situations.

Children of different ages
▲ Toddlers are too young to have strong opinions about what they would like to be, but they love to role-play familiar scenarios such as Mummies and Daddies and going to see the doctor! Encourage this with suitable props and dressing-up clothes.
▲ Going into role with older children will help them to appreciate more than just the obvious aspects of the job in question.

Jobs on the go

As a starting-point, when you are out and about with the children, look at all the different places where people work, from hospitals, police stations and shops, to dentists, libraries and hairdressers. The children will also see bus, lorry, taxi and train drivers. Just the jobs for getting around and seeing people!

What to do
● Build your own taxi using a large cardboard box. Challenge the children to paint or glue on some accessories, such as mirrors, lights and switches. Encourage them to role-play taking fares, choosing destinations and pretending to spot things out of their 'windows'!

● If the children would rather be plane, bus or train drivers, then simply assemble a row of chairs and let their imaginations do the rest – do not forget to fasten seatbelts!

Retail therapy

Children's ideas of shop work are often focused on using a till and handling money. As they role-play working in a shop, you can help them to learn about stocking shelves, speaking to customers and keeping the shop tidy as well!

What to do
● Let the children set up and run their own 'corner shop', using tins from the cupboard and empty boxes to put on display. Older children will understand the principles of paying for things and giving change. Encourage the use of play money and

practise counting with the children.

● Set up a shoe shop. Challenge the children to match several pairs of shoes, put them in shoeboxes and write on their sizes. Make a foot measurer out of cardboard (mark on some measurements with a ruler) and help pairs of children to measure each other's feet.

Building sights

There are plenty of different building jobs, and they are not all about laying bricks. Encourage the children to think about other related jobs, such as electricians, plumbers and decorators.

What to do

● Take a tour around your home. Show the children pipes, light switches, brick walls, garden plants and painted or papered walls. Talk about all the different jobs that are

Further ideas

▲ Arrange to visit some places of work, such as a fire station, library and shop.
▲ Find out about all the different types of caring profession, from nurses to vets.
▲ Encourage the children to use small world toys to act out the roles of the different emergency services, from ambulances, to breakdown vehicles.

involved with each of these things.

● Pretend to plan a decorating job with the children. Look through a home-improvements catalogue together and talk about all the things that you would need to do the job. If possible, visit a DIY store.

● Take part in some building-work role-play. Provide toy tool kits and imagine that you are fixing or improving a room in your home!

That's entertainment

Singing, dancing, acting – many people first demonstrate a flair for entertaining when they are very young. If you have a dressing-up box, it will come into its own while the children act out their favourite fairy tales and nursery rhymes.

What to do

● Choose a favourite fairy tale or nursery rhyme, provide some dressing-up clothes and rehearse a simple scene from it. Plan to put on a little show for the children's parents when they come to collect them.

● Some children are very shy about performing, but do not forget there are plenty of behind the scenes roles to fulfil, from making props, costumes and scenery to designing and producing tickets.

Top tips

▲ Keep a well-stocked dressing-up box for the children to use.
▲ Get out into the community as often as you can, to see the different types of work that people do.
▲ Make sure that the children understand that you do important work too!

Resource bank

Story and picture books

● *Well Done, Little Bear* by Martin Waddell (Walker Books). The story of a little bear's first big adventure out in the woods.
● *Let's Go, Anna!* by Vivian French and Alex Ayliffe (David and Charles Children's Books). Anna and her dad go shopping, but can they remember what is on the shopping list?
● *Lucy & Tom at the Seaside* by Shirley Hughes (Picture Puffin). Lucy and Tom enjoy a day at the seaside building a sandcastle, finding crabs in a rock-pool, making seaweed faces in the sand and riding a donkey on the beach.

Information books

● *Fun with Nature* by Cecilia Fitzsimons (Southwater). Bark-rubbing, leaf-painting, pebble pictures – lots of ideas to enhance your nature walks.
● *Weather* by Sally Hewitt (Franklin Watts) uses simple terms to introduce children to the science surrounding weather.

Equipment

● Have a minibeast safari – collect clean empty jam jars and a magnifying glass and take a stroll around the garden or the local park to see the wide range of bugs and other creatures that live there. Do not forget to put creatures and their habitats back exactly as you found them.
● Make sure that you always have spares of suncream, sun-hats, umbrellas and wellington boots!

Websites

● www.wizziwiz.co.uk
Includes a comprehensive listing of tourist attractions, sporting events and nature destinations in all areas of the country.
● www.getnature.co.uk
Includes links to sites about every type of nature topic imaginable, from birds and butterflies to fish and flowers.
● www.farmsforschools.org.uk
Contains a directory of farms that have facilities for school visits, organised by county.
● www.goodbeachguide.co.uk
Provides information on safe, clean beaches.

Places to visit

● Visit **Legoland**, in Windsor, Berkshire, and the children will come back full of ideas for their own LEGO modelling sessions. Tel: 0870-504 0404.
● Visit **Denver Windmill** in West Norfolk. Built in 1835, the mill continued to grind corn using wind power for over one hundred years. Now it has been restored to full working order and flour is once again being milled using the power of the wind. Tel: 01366-384 009.
● Visit a real life farm such as **Noah's Ark Farm Centre** in Bristol, where children can meet up to 34 animal species, enjoy tractor rides and have fun in the two adventure playgrounds. Tel: 01275-852 606.
● Contact your local countryside ranger service or tourist information office for details of local guided walks.

Arts and crafts

Whether it involves painting simple abstract colours and shapes on to a piece of paper, or producing complex, elaborate junk models, children of all ages love to be creative. This chapter will look at a range of art and craft activities, using lots of household materials, that are designed to keep children absorbed and entertained for hours.

Why arts and crafts?

Children love being able to make things that they can show, and they gain a great deal of satisfaction when their products are put on display. In being creative, they are developing their imagination and ability to express themselves. Activities can be abstract, stemming from the children's own ideas, or themed, which will involve more planning and requires them to give a little more thought to what they are doing. In organising these activities, your role is to supervise and encourage their ideas, but also to know when to let them try some of them on their own. Whether or not they go on to become artists, they will have plenty of fun along the way!

A range of ages

Art and craft activities help develop hand–eye co-ordination and manual dexterity. For very young children, simply exploring the textures and colours of different materials they are using, such as fabrics, yarns and papers, promotes these skills and gives them a broader idea of the world around them. Older children can use these activities to develop a natural artistic flair, and even those who do not feel naturally artistic will find something they enjoy making.

Special advice

Craft play is educational and fun, however, issues such as planning, safety and tidying up are just as important and are also covered in this chapter. Parents and carers will also be able to develop a sense of when children need extra supervision and when to let them work things out on their own.

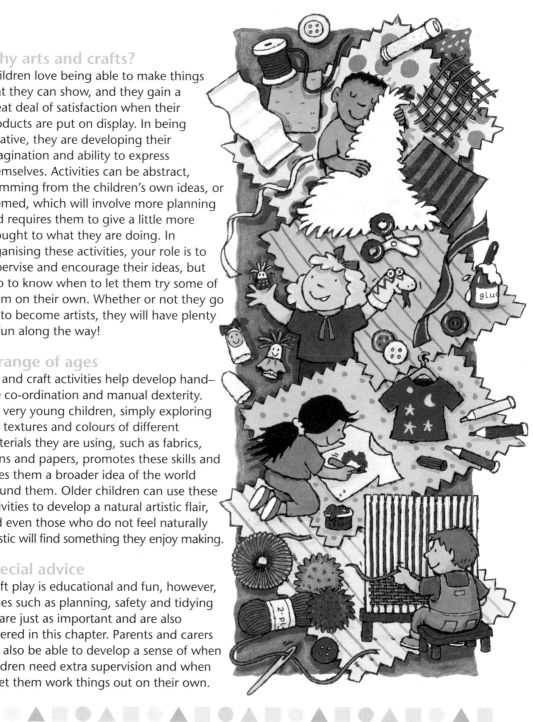

Make your own music

Music is an important part of a child's development. From an early age, children are readily stimulated by the sound of music – even young babies 'dance' to the sound of a familiar tune! The ideas in this chapter will provide you with some practical tips for making simple music and musical instruments with the children.

Children of different ages

▲ Challenge older children to play well-known tunes with their home-made instruments.

▲ Toddlers and babies will enjoy making simple music with household objects, such as banging two saucepan lids together, or banging bowls and saucepans with a wooden spoon!

Rhythm all around

Whether it is the drum beat in a favourite pop song, a clock tick-tocking in a room or the distinctive beat of your own heart, rhythms are everywhere. The following ideas give suggestions for ways to 'beat it' together!

What to do

● Read out favourite poems and nursery rhymes, such as 'Humpty Dumpty', emphasising the natural rhythm of the words in each line.

● Create your own rhythms with some home-made percussion instruments (see page 27).

Going outdoors

▲ Make some garden rhythms by shaking pebbles in buckets and sweeping sand and water around a patio!

▲ If you are in the car on a rainy day, turn on the windscreen wipers and count the beats together, as they swish from side to side.

● Listen for rhythms in everyday sounds, such as the ticking clock, the washing machine drum, the bubbling saucepan and so on.

Percussion instruments

There is nothing children like better than trying out new instruments. With a little help and imagination they can make some of their own percussion instruments.

What to do

● Maracas – Provide each child with an empty plastic bottle and lid. Fill the bottle with some lentils or dried peas. Screw the lid on tightly. Decorate the side of the bottle by gluing on pieces of coloured foil or painted paper. Make sure that young children do not put the small pieces in their mouths, or up their noses!

● Rainbow xylophone – Fill five or six empty glass bottles with varying amounts of water. Place them in a line from the smallest to the largest amount of water. Add a different food colouring/ink or paint to each one to make a rainbow xylophone! Let the children make some music by gently tapping the bottles with a wooden spoon.

String instruments

Violins, guitars and cellos are all string instruments which can be plucked in order to produce musical notes. Their designs are very similar, and can be replicated, in simple forms by using just a few household objects.

What to do

● Create a simple string instrument by placing large elastic bands around the outside of an empty shoebox. The children can pluck at the elastic bands to make a sound.

● Make a guitar with older children using a shoebox, the hollow tube from a roll of foil and some thin elastic. Cut a circle in the lid of the shoebox and another in one end of the shoebox. Attach the lid to the shoebox using firm sticky tape. Push the tube through the circle in the end and then cut a 2cm slit on both sides of the top of the tube. Knot the elastic and pass it through the slit, pass it down the front of the guitar, over the middle circle and up the back of the box to be fastened off in the slit at the back of the tube. When the elastic is plucked, the guitar will produce a realistic sound.

Wind instruments

Young children are likely to be familiar with some wind instruments, such as trumpets and recorders. You can explain to older children that sound is produced when you blow into the instrument, causing air to vibrate inside the mouthpiece.

What to do

● Make a simple wind instrument with a cardboard tube and a paper drinking straw. Flatten one end of the straw and cut the corners to make a pointed shape. This will be the reed which produces the sound. Cut out a card circle, to make a lid over the end of the tube. Make a small hole for the straw to be pushed through the lid, leaving the reed end sticking out. Attach the lid and straw securely with sticky tape. Let the children blow down the straw to produce a sound!

● Try using different widths and lengths of cardboard tubing and listen to the different sounds of the notes.

● Let the children decorate their wind instruments with paint or sticky paper to make them more attractive.

Top tips

▲ Keep a stockpile of empty tubes, boxes, card and other types of packaging.

▲ Make sure that toddlers and babies are not left unsupervised when handling small objects.

▲ Make some home-made drumsticks by fixing blobs of Plasticine around the ends of blunt pencils!

TICK TOCK

Celebrating craft

Arts and crafts have played an important part in people's lives for centuries. They are a way of recording or preserving different aspects of everyday lives and cultures, and also provide hours of pleasure as hobbies and pastimes. Why not take a look at some of the more traditional crafts and where they came from?

Material world

All arts and craft activities start with the raw materials, and we are surrounded by many different varieties; from fabrics and yarns, to plastics and papers. But where do they come from, and how are they made?

What to do

● Explain the difference between natural and manufactured fibres. Use books to explore where natural fibres such as wool and cotton come from.
● Use children's sculpting clay to show how different-shaped objects, such as plates and bowls, can be formed and baked in the oven.
● Plait lengths of coloured wool together to make a strong yarn, which can then be used to decorate models, puppets or as a hair decoration.

Crafts on display

Although children love to try their hand at new crafts, they will enjoy watching the experts at work. Take advantage of opportunities to see, up close, some of our oldest country crafts, as well as the more modern techniques.

Talk about

▲ What animals, beside sheep, provide fur or hair that can be woven?
▲ If you had no craft materials, how would you make a picture that you could leave behind for other people to look at?

Where to go

● Local craft fairs or touring exhibitions of traditional crafts, such as 'corn dollying' and 'wood turning', are ideal for seeing how elaborate shapes can be produced from simple raw materials.
● Try to find a local working mill that produces textiles or wool, to experience how some of the raw materials that you are using have been made.
● Look at other local examples of craft work, such as statues around the town, stonework on old buildings and stained-glass windows in a church. Look out for modern examples, such as sculptures in civic buildings or public parks.

Crafts around the world

Different countries have their own traditional crafts, and it is interesting to look at how some of them have developed and how long ago they were created.

What to do

● Origami is the art of paper folding – no scissors and no glue – and it began hundreds of years ago in Japan. The simplest way to demonstrate this is by making paper aeroplanes.

● Tie-dying is a craft that creates a marbled effect on dyed cloth. It is very popular in parts of Africa. Crumple a piece of plain cloth into a very tight ball, secure with string or elastic bands, and submerge in a bowl of water coloured with food colouring. After 15 minutes, remove the cloth and untie to see some interesting results.

● Mexican dough is quick to make and good for small mouldings. Tear two or three slices of white bread into small pieces and mix in a bowl with one tablespoon of white glue, and two teaspoons of glycerine to form a dough. Knead well and cover with cling film for 30 minutes. Use it fairly quickly to make small models and then bake them at 180°C for about half an hour.

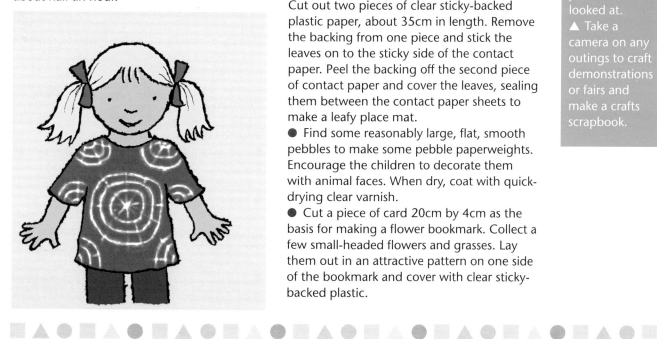

● Make paper 'lace' by folding a circle of white paper into quarters. Cut lots of different shapes and edgings into and around the circle, and unfold to reveal a 'lace' place mat.

Seasonal nature crafts

Venture outdoors and collect a range of natural craft materials, such as fallen leaves, pine cones and so on. These will vary according to the seasons, but can be used to produce some beautiful designs.

What to do

● Collect different coloured autumn leaves. Cut out two pieces of clear sticky-backed plastic paper, about 35cm in length. Remove the backing from one piece and stick the leaves on to the sticky side of the contact paper. Peel the backing off the second piece of contact paper and cover the leaves, sealing them between the contact paper sheets to make a leafy place mat.

● Find some reasonably large, flat, smooth pebbles to make some pebble paperweights. Encourage the children to decorate them with animal faces. When dry, coat with quick-drying clear varnish.

● Cut a piece of card 20cm by 4cm as the basis for making a flower bookmark. Collect a few small-headed flowers and grasses. Lay them out in an attractive pattern on one side of the bookmark and cover with clear sticky-backed plastic.

Top tips

▲ Use a globe or atlas with older children to point out the various countries that produce some of the crafts you have looked at.

▲ Take a camera on any outings to craft demonstrations or fairs and make a crafts scrapbook.

CHAPTER

2

Arts and crafts

Junk modelling

What may look like items of junk for the recycling bin can easily be turned into a child's work of art. Junk modelling is fun to do, especially when children have something to show at the end of it. Keep a large cardboard box to store your junk, which can be anything from cereal boxes and kitchen roll tubes, to yoghurt pots and egg boxes. For detailed decoration, collect old lolly sticks, bubble wrap, old balls of wool and foil cases from pies and tarts.

Children of different ages

▲ Older children may want to produce more elaborate designs for their models – make sure you provide plenty of decorative materials.
▲ Cut out pictures from magazines for smaller children to copy from.

On the go!

Large boxes used to package items such as televisions and washing machines are ideal for making cars, buses, and aeroplanes – in other words, models that children can really get into!

What to do
Provide large boxes for the children to use and cut doors large enough for children to open them. Include as many realistic gadgets made from junk materials as you can, such as speedometers and petrol gauges.
● Stick two or three large boxes together and make a model bus that can fit two or three little people inside!
● Have a competition to see who can make the best spaceship.

Mini models

Miniature models are a little fiddlier to make and younger children will need extra help, but children will love making scaled-down models of their bedroom, the garden or even a mini zoo.

What to do
● Recreate a room using small boxes such as shoeboxes. Decorate them using any leftover wallpaper.
● Make an entire town using old boxes and cartons, paper, crayons, tape, and glue. Start by creating the basic shapes and then encourage the children to add finer details using the craft and collage materials.
● Start a collection of model cars made from small cereal boxes.

Marvellous mobiles

Children especially love making models that can be put on display. Mobiles, which they can hang in their bedrooms, range from simple designs to more elaborate themed ideas.

What to do
● Paint several empty yoghurt pots in different colours. Push an opened paper clip through the bottom and bend it over to stop it slipping out. Attach the pots to chains of paper clips, and hang them from metal coat hanger wires (ensuring that they are safely out of the reach of young children).
● Make a mobile of the solar system complete with the Sun and its nine planets. Mix a large bowlful of paste for papier-mâché models and form nine balls – roughly 5 to 7cm in diameter, and one larger ball of 10cm for the Sun (painted yellow). Leave to dry and then paint – for example, Mars red, Earth blue and Jupiter with orange stripes around the middle. Use a pipe cleaner or florist's wire to make a circular frame, approximately 20cm in diameter, with a central crosswire. Attach the large yellow Sun to the middle of the frame using dark wool, and the nine planets in circular orbits around it (see the diagram on page 43 for the names and order of the planets).

Boat modelling

Invite the children to build model boats out of junk and test them in a large bowl, bath or paddling pool, filled with a few inches of water. Which materials will float? Which will become waterlogged and sink to the bottom? The children will have fun finding out.

What to do
● Use plastic milk and soft drink containers, cut in half lengthways, to make boats. Add drinking straws and paper to make sails.
● Foil dishes from cakes and pies make excellent sailing boats. They can be moulded into different shapes and decorated.
● Have a boat race. Line up two or three boats with sails and use drinking straws to blow them along.

Further ideas
▲ Find out whether there are any local modelling competitions at the library or museum during the school holidays.
▲ Try using some more challenging materials such as chicken wire and plaster of Paris.

Top tips
▲ Boost your junk collection by asking friends and neighbours to collect as well.
▲ A large sheet of plastic placed on the floor under the table where you are working will be easy to clean and will prevent tiny bits of junk from messing up the room.
▲ Use child-friendly glue that is non-toxic and will not stick their fingers together.
▲ Use a clear varnish to coat the papier-mâché mobiles – it gives a smooth, shiny finish and they will last longer.
▲ More ambitious modelling projects will take longer to complete. Make sure that you have somewhere safe to keep unfinished models.

■●▲■●▲■●▲■●▲■●▲■●▲■●▲■

True colours

Colour is vital for children's early identification skills, and experimenting with it in craft and play activities provides fascinating fun as well as opportunities for learning.

Children of different ages
▲ Play simple games of 'I spy' using colours, or try spotting cars by their colour, to help toddlers and young children to identify and remember their colours.
▲ Older children can be taught to remember the colours of the rainbow using simple rhymes or memory devices, such as the well-known phrase 'Richard of York gained battles in vain'.

Pure colour

Older children will be fascinated to learn that all the colours that we see come from white light. At this age it is best not to baffle them with science, but they will enjoy having their curiosity stimulated with some fun experiments and craft activities.

white light

What to do
● Provide some black and white photographs for the children to look at. Compare them to some colour photographs and notice how much more information the colour images give us.
● Make a spinner to demonstrate the principle of white light. Cut out a circle of white card, about 6cm in diameter and mark out 12 segments. Colour each segment a colour of the spectrum (except indigo, as this is a mix of blue and violet). Repeat the colour

pattern until all the segments have been coloured in. Push a cocktail stick through the centre of the circle and spin it as fast as possible. As the circle spins, the colours will merge to make a creamy white.
● Make some spinners using two colours, such as red and blue. See what colours they make as they are spun.

Making rainbows

Explain simply to the children that when the sun shines on a rainy day, white sunlight may pass through the raindrops and be broken down into the colours of the spectrum to form a rainbow.

What to do
● To make your own rainbow, place a bowl or tank of water on a table in front of a light coloured wall. Position a small hand mirror in the water, at an angle, trying to create a triangular-shaped section of water between the mirror and the edge of the tank. Move the mirror carefully until you see a rainbow reflected on the wall.
● Young children need little encouragement to have a bubble-blowing session! Show them how to make rainbows by gently blowing on the bubbles they have made to make them bend in and out. You could explain to older children that as the surface of the bubble bends in and out, the light shining through it is broken up, making a rainbow appear on the bubble's surface.

Further ideas
▲ Cut out brightly coloured pictures from magazines and sort them by their predominant colours. Use them to make some beautiful colour collages.
▲ Look out for ways in which colour is used to identify things, such as how football teams play in different coloured strips to avoid confusion and how traffic lights use colours to control traffic on the roads.

Mixing colours

Children are delighted to make the discovery that if they mix some of the primary colours (red, yellow and blue) together they can create new colours!

What to do

● Start by letting the children experiment with mixing poster paint colours together. What results do they achieve?

● Create some unusual effects by mixing coloured light. Shine white torchlight through sheets of different coloured Cellophane on to a white surface. Try overlapping different colours of paper to produce secondary light colours.

● Let the children make their own coloured torchlight by sticking sheets of coloured Cellophane over the end of the torch. Suggest that they try shining this light on to different coloured objects and surfaces to see what happens.

Camouflage

Children are fascinated to find out about how animals use their special colours and markings to hide themselves from others. Colourful and geometric animal patterns can be used for the basis of some creative and attractive artwork.

What to do

● Draw and cut out some animal shapes – anything from fish to zebras! Draw coloured stripes or spots on their bodies. On separate pieces of paper, draw the same markings. Now colour some of the animal cut-outs in different colours. Place the animal cut-outs on top of the sheets of painted paper to show how camouflage works. Let younger children experiment simply by making spotty and stripy marks on their paper.

● Make underwater pictures using paint and collage materials. Cut out some tissue paper weeds and anemones and partially stick them down on to the paper. Cut out some fish shapes and paint them the same colour as the weeds and anemones. Hide the fish to make an underwater camouflage scene!

Top tips

▲ Transparent coloured sweet wrappers make a cheap and effective substitute for sheets of Cellophane.

▲ Plastic, nine hole paint palettes give the children plenty of scope for colour mixing and are easy to clean afterwards.

Children of different ages

▲ Let older children be more adventurous with their papier-mâché models. For example, small pieces of chicken wire can be moulded into more complex shapes and a number of small cardboard boxes can be glued together to make cars and buildings. These shapes can be covered in the same way and painted.

▲ Most toddlers and babies love hands-on messy activities and delight in the sensation of handling the materials as much as they do in the finished results of their work!

Messy play

It is not often that we encourage children to make a mess – in fact most of the time we seem to do just the opposite! But there are occasions when messy play can have an important role in developing the children's co-ordination and stimulating their imaginations.

Papier mâché

This is a perennial favourite with children. The easiest way to start working with papier mâché is to find an object to cover. Balloons are ideal for making animals and head shapes. Boxes, plates, bowls and any unusually shaped objects are also good to use as a base.

Step by step

● The paste – mix equal parts of flour and water in a bowl to make a smooth paste.

● The strips – cut out plenty of strips of newspaper – about 2cm wide. The children then paint the glue on to the strips and smooth them in a layer on to their mould (bowl, balloon, and so on). Once the first layer is dry they can begin a second layer, and so on until the right thickness is reached.

● Finishing touches – once the final shape is finished and dry, add any extra pieces that are needed. Cut out bits of cardboard to make ears and legs and fix them down with sticky tape. Add another layer of papier mâché to cover the join. Once the whole model is completely dry it can be painted and decorated!

Water play

Water is the simplest and cheapest of materials with which children can mess around. Collect a variety of plastic containers, as well as a number of household items, such as spoons, plastic cups and other measuring tools.

Further ideas

▲ Keep a collection of old magazines and catalogues. Look through them with the children, pick a theme, cut out the pictures and help them to make a collage picture.

▲ Make your own finger-paints with this simple recipe: mix half a cup of cornflour and two cups of water in a saucepan. Boil the mixture until it thickens. Allow to cool, then pour into jars or other storage containers and colour with food colouring. The paints work best on glossy paper.

about. Open the sheet up and let their imaginations run wild as they try to describe what objects and images they see in their finished paintings.

● Drop a few blobs of poster paint on to a clean sheet of paper. Invite the children to use drinking straws to blow on the blobs to make long streaks of paint. They will make some wonderful coloured patterns!

Top tips
▲ Before starting any messy activities make sure you have plenty of cloths, towels and plastic aprons handy.
▲ A plastic sheet on the floor around the area in which you are working will help to contain any spillages.
▲ If you are using your own dishes as moulds for papier mâché, cover them in cling film or foil first, for easy removal.
▲ Encourage the children to help with the clearing up. They will then begin to appreciate why messy days are a special treat!

What to do

● Children love to paint water, or a mixture of water and sand, on garden paving and walls, using paintbrushes. Older children may paint the letters of their names, while younger children will be content with making simple patterns using long brush strokes and then watching them evaporate in the sun.

● An empty squeezy bottle offers endless ideas for water play. See who can squirt a water jet the furthest or the highest. Encourage the children to write letters, numbers and words using the water bottle.

Painting

Forget the paintbrushes and spatulas, try some adventurous finger- and blow-painting!

What to do

● Let the children finger-paint some abstract creations on to a blank sheet of paper. Fold it in half and rub firmly to spread the paint

Gloop, slime and gunge!

What could be more fun than being allowed to squish, squeeze and mix? Children of all ages can get messy and creative with these slimy ideas.

What to do

● Fill a tray with jelly for babies and toddlers to explore! Watch it wobble and slide, then take a handful to squeeze and squish! Can you roll it in a ball? Can you squeeze it through your fingers?

● Make a play slime by blending cornflour, water and food colouring into a thick paste. The mixture is slimy when you squish it between your fingers, but feels hard if you try and punch it!

Paper play

Where would we be without paper? We use it for so many things every day – for reading, writing and drawing; for wrapping up birthday presents; for mopping up spillages, and for packaging food. But aside from being extremely useful, paper can provide hours of fun.

Children of different ages

▲ Older children might want to make something that can be used in the house, such as place mats – so try to provide plenty of alternative decorative materials.

▲ Young children and toddlers will need closer supervision, but should be encouraged to express their ideas clearly.

Safety matters

▲ Make sure small children are supervised during cutting and gluing activities.

▲ Ensure that the children use safety scissors.

▲ Paper can cut – take care when using copier paper.

▲ Keep glitter or small pieces of sticky paper away from the children's eyes, they can be irritants.

Paper crafts

There are many different types of paper that can be used for crafts, from delicate crêpe to heavy duty cardboard. Old computer printer paper and newspaper also come in handy for paper play activities.

What to do

● Grow paper palm trees by rolling two or three sheets of newspaper into a tube and fastening with sticky tape. Cut three or four slits down the side of the tube, push the bottom of the tube up and pull the 'leaves' out from the top.

● Invite the children to make handprints on crêpe paper, then cut these out and make handprint flowers.

Experiments with paper

Different types of paper are used for different things – some are stronger than others, while some are more absorbent. Try some of these easy experiments to find out exactly what different papers can do.

What to do

● Cut out strips of newspaper, tissue paper, drawing paper, and thin card. Go outside and fill a bucket with some sand or water. Test which strip of paper can be used to lift the bucket.

● Half-fill a jar with coloured water. Use paper clips to attach strips of different types of paper to straws. Note how absorbent the different strips of paper are by dipping them into the water. Older children can measure how quickly each one soaks up the water and how far the water travels up the strip.

● Corrugate paper by making 1cm folds in alternate directions, creating a concertina effect. Rest the folded paper across a bowl of water and test its strength by placing objects on it.

Paper masks

Children can really let their imaginations run wild when they start making their own masks. From a basic oval, cut out of sturdy white card, secured with elastic at the sides, they can turn themselves into jungle animals, circus performers or even alien visitors from outer space!

What to do

● Use basic oval mask templates and become clowns! Paint with bright poster paints for the facial make up and stick on tufts of red or orange wool around the sides for the hair.

● Cut several strands of brown or black wool into 1cm pieces. Coat the front of a basic mask with glue and stick on the wool pieces. Stick a pair of large paper ears on the side of the mask and you can be a chimpanzee!

● Cover an oval mask with aluminium foil and decorate with shiny toffee wrappers to make an authentic spaceman.

Stamp art

Printing on paper can create beautiful patterns and designs, and is so easy that young toddlers will be able to manage this on their own. There are lots of things that can be used to make the stamps, including fruit, vegetables and household sponges.

What to do

● Find different shapes, sizes and types of leaves to dip into paint and make prints from.

● Make printed trails of hand or footprints using a shallow tray of powder paint and a large roll of paper, such as unwanted wallpaper.

● Dip the wheels of a small toy car into the paint bath and drive it across the paper to leave tyre tracks.

The paper cycle

Children may be surprised to learn that paper starts out as a living thing, and can be recycled to conserve the trees that provide it. Conservation and the environment are important issues for children to learn about and the paper cycle is an excellent example to use.

What to do

● Use library books to explain where paper comes from and how it is made.

● Make your own paper pulp by mixing finely chopped newspaper with water and spreading it in very thin layers on to sheets of plastic (such as waste bin liners). When these are dry, they can be peeled off the plastic carefully and printed on all over again.

● Talk about recycling. Look around the house for waste paper that can be reused and visit your local recycling station.

Top tips

▲ Save all your Sunday magazines – they often have some of the most interesting things to cut out.

▲ Keep an A3 folder to store finished pictures.

Make–believe play

It seems there is no limit to a child's imagination, which may be why they are experts at make–believe play. Whether it is a favourite television programme or story that inspires them, they love stepping into the role of a favourite character. Imaginative play also gives children a sense of control as they interpret the dramas of everyday life and practice the rules of social behaviour.

Children of different ages

▲ Some children are more self-conscious than others and this is often more apparent around the ages of seven or eight. They should be encouraged, but not pressurised into taking part in role-play.
▲ Younger children love to mimic, copying animal noises and activities that they see older children doing, and this should be encouraged.

Dressing-up

Children find it hard to resist the magic of the dressing-up box, and it does not have to be filled with expensive replica outfits. Hats, bags, belts and old cardigans or shirts can easily be turned into a variety of outfits, while the children's imagination will do the rest.

What to do

● Create some role-play settings, such as 'at the shops', 'in the classroom' or 'on an aeroplane'. Invite the children to dress up to go into role and suggest some imaginary storylines for them to act out, such as 'What shall I buy for dinner today?' or 'What

Safety matters

▲ Make sure the face paints you use are good quality and conform to British Safety Standards. Check with parents first, and try a little patch on the back of their hands beforehand.
▲ Young children need close supervision when using glue and when decorating with glitter, sequins, wool and so on.

happens when the captain of the ship cannot find the map?'.

● Think of some popular nursery rhymes, such as 'Little Bo Peep', or 'The Grand Old Duke of York', and let the children act them out in costume.

● If you do not have a large collection of hats, let the children make some of their own. All you need is some coloured card, glue, and paints. Keep it simple. Make a card band that fits around the head and then create any design you like, such as a soldier's hat or a pirate's cap that can be cut out and stuck on to the front of the headband.

Puppets

Puppet shows have always been a favourite with children, from Punch and Judy to Sooty and Sweep. They see them as simply another way of acting out stories, developing characters and allowing their imagination to run free.

What to do

● The easiest puppets to make are glove or finger puppets. Find an old pair of woollen gloves and decorate each of the fingers as different characters, using bits of wool, fabric and felt-tipped pens.

● Shadow puppets do not require any materials, but you will need a bright lamp or torch and a plain white or light-coloured wall on which to project the shadows. Show the children how to make animal shapes with their hands – dogs, rabbits and even snakes. Make them talk by synchronising speech with movement of the shadow puppet's mouth.

● Use a few old socks to create a family of sock puppets that can be decorated with felt-tipped pens, glitter and wool.

Funny faces

Children love having their faces painted – it gives them a real sense of being something or somebody else and provides an opportunity to play out some exciting roles.

What to do

● Make a lion's den using a couple of blankets draped over two or three chairs and paint the children's faces with simple stripes and whiskers. Encourage them to practise their roars and make lion movements such as stalking prey or flopping lazily in the sunshine.

● Children will love to have their faces painted up as clowns – the funnier the better. Add a few simple props such as a ball and a pogo stick for older children.

Who am I?

Charades is an activity for children of all ages, as the repertoire of characters and objects to choose to be is endless. Playing charades helps children to develop observation skills while providing hours of fun for the performers.

What to do

● Choose a theme, such as jobs, television programmes, books and so on – whatever is appropriate for the age and interests of the children. Write a few examples of each on pieces of paper. Either whisper the word to the child, or give it to them to read. Ask them to mime while the rest of you try to guess who or what they are trying to be.

● Do the same again, this time with the theme of animals that make a noise, such as a donkey, a dog or a cat.

Resource bank

Story and picture books
● *Katie Meets the Impressionists* by James Mayhew (Orchard Books). Katie enjoys a visit to an art gallery when five of the Impressionist paintings come to life.
● *Strawberries Are Red* by Petr Horacek (Walker Books). This ingenious and stylish board book, an introduction to colours, contains a glorious surprise at the end!

Information books
● *Amazing Faces and Disguises* (Lorenz Books) contains dozens of ideas for masks, fancy dress and face painting to create wonderful disguises.
● *Kids Create* by Lauri Carlson (Williamson Publishing Co) has lots of ideas from box-modelling to potato-printing.
● *What Shall I Draw?*, *What Shall I Paint?* and *What Shall I Make?* (all Usborne) provide simple, yet effective creative ideas to capture young children's imaginations.

Equipment
● Save old Christmas and birthday cards to cut out and make personalised stationery, gift tags and collages.
● Keep chunky, plastic, safety scissors handy to let young children have their first try at cutting out in safety.
● Buy some modelling clay, available from specialist art and craft suppliers, to make sculptures or pieces of crockery that can be fired in the oven.

Websites
● www.magic-factory.co.uk
This activity website offers an assortment of online games that use light and colour for children aged up to eight years.
● www.activityvillage.co.uk
A site full of ideas for crafts and activities for children of all ages.

Places to visit
● Visit the **Royal Crown Derby Visitors Centre** to see craftsmen at work making Royal Crown Derby. The centre includes factory tours, a demonstration studio, museum and factory shop. Tel: 01332-712 800.
● A visit to the **National Museum of Photography, Film & Television** in Bradford, West Yorkshire, will mean a day full of exploration of how television and film were invented – how they use light and colour and some of the modern techniques. Tel: 01274-202 030.
● Visit your local art gallery and museum to take a look at a range of artefacts, sculptures and paintings. Join any available mailing lists to find out about special events for children and art in your area.

Whatever path children choose to take in later life, a sound grasp of words and numbers will help them on their way. In addition to helping develop those vital skills, the activities in this chapter will teach children that words and numbers can be fun.

Numbers and words

Why 'Numbers and words'?

There is no getting away from the fact that we use words and numbers in almost every aspect of our lives, and it is through everyday activities that children can begin to appreciate how important they are. Children with good reading skills tend to be more inquisitive about the world around them, and good numeracy skills provide an excellent foundation upon which to develop skills in computers and science. Most experts in childhood development agree that the earlier children are introduced to numbers and words (in the context of play), the easier they will find the topics as they progress through school and into adult life. An introduction to literacy and numeracy skills through lively and interesting activities will set them on the road to a lifetime of enjoyment.

A range of ages

Basic numeracy and literacy can be introduced from a very early age. Even before they can talk, young babies enjoy listening to words and the rhythms that words make in stories and poetry, and can become absorbed in watching the process of counting. Toddlers and young children should be encouraged to describe what they see around them, and talk about stories that have been read to them. They can be introduced to simple activities that require addition and subtraction. Older children will benefit from any additional number and word activities in order to build on what they are beginning to learn at school.

Special advice

Keep words and number activities short and simple, especially for younger children who tend to have shorter attention spans and can easily lose interest. Keep word and number activities fun! Do not try to present number and word activities in a formal teaching style – the children have plenty of classroom years ahead of them for that!

Seeing stars

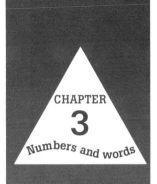

Children are endlessly fascinated by the theme of space, whether it is the latest *Star Wars* film, or the sight of a full moon on a clear evening. From exploring shapes to comparing the sizes of the planets, there is a lot of mathematics to be found in the topic. The following ideas provide suggestions for some cosmically cool activities.

Children of different ages

▲ Babies and toddlers love things that sparkle and enjoy comforting and familiar tunes, such as 'Twinkle, Twinkle, Little Star' (Traditional).
▲ Older children may want to learn more about the way the Earth moves, and how close we are to the other planets. It is worth borrowing some books on the topic from the library to help you to answer their questions.

Star shapes

The apparent changing shape of the Moon, traditional star shapes, spherical planets and planets with 'rings' around them, all provide great starting-points for some interesting work on shapes.

What to do

● Watch the Moon on a regular basis with the children on winter evenings. Start with a full Moon and watch how it changes shape over a few weeks. Talk about the different shapes with the children. Encourage younger children to simply notice the change, and ask

older children to try and draw the different shapes they see to make a 'Moon log book'.
● Cut out some card star, planet, moon and sun templates for the children to draw round. Suggest that older children use them to make pictures of the galaxy!
● Look at pictures of the stars, constellations and the planets. Talk about the different shapes together.

Size and distance

Young children are fascinated to learn that beyond the Moon are the planets of the solar system, all different colours and sizes, and taking different amounts of time to travel around the Sun.

What to do

● Enlist the children's help to make a simple wall frieze of the nine planets and their relative distances from the Sun. Use a length of old wallpaper painted black as the background. Ask the children to cut out and colour the different planets. Talk about the different comparative sizes, starting with the biggest and working down. Then talk about the relative distances from the Sun, starting with the nearest and progressing to the furthest. Stick the planet and Sun pictures in place to make your frieze.

Further ideas

▲ Find some pictures and illustrations of the Moon's surfaces and, using modelling clay or papier mâché, let the children make their own moonscapes, complete with rocks and craters.
▲ If you have access to a small telescope or binoculars, wrap up warm and head for the garden to do some real star-gazing before the children go home.

● Older children might be interested to read the actual distances that the planets are from the Sun and each other, and find out how long it would take to reach them in a rocket. A good children's space encyclopaedia, such as *Enyclopedia of Space and the Universe* (Dorling Kindersley), should provide the necessary mind-boggling facts and figures!

Patterns

Early astronomers studied the stars in the sky and created the constellations, images and characters formed by drawing imaginary lines between adjacent stars. Some of the easiest constellations to spot include the Plough, the Big Dipper and Orion, with the three characteristic stars that form Orion's Belt.

What to do

● Create your own indoor version of the sky at night – let the children design their constellation, marking out the main points or stars on a piece of black card or paper. Use the sharp end of a pair of scissors to make holes where the stars have been marked. Turn off the lights and shine a torch behind the paper – the only light that will shine through will be the constellations.
● Make some wax resist paintings of the sky at night. Ask the children to each use a yellow wax crayon to mark a pattern of stars on a piece of white paper. Then invite them to brush over it with black paint to create the night sky, with yellow stars shining through!

Top tips

▲ The nine planets appear in the following order (in terms of distance from the Sun): Mercury, Venus, Earth, Mars, Jupiter, Saturn, Uranus, Neptune and Pluto.
▲ Once children get into the space theme they will probably be eager to make their own spaceship models! Make sure you have plenty of glue and different-shaped boxes to cope with the rush!
▲ Remember, the easiest planet to see is Venus, which often appears as a very bright object above the horizon in the early evening.

Measure for pleasure

Whether it's the distance on a road sign or the amount of flour in a cake, life is full of different measurements. Even very young children can grasp principles such as 'bigger' and 'heavier', while older ones soon become familiar with standard units such as litres and kilometres. So get out your ruler, kitchen scales and measuring jug, and start measuring for fun.

Children of different ages
▲ Babies and toddlers will be learning about size, shape and space as they fill and empty pots, bowls and containers with water and other substances and objects.
▲ Younger children will enjoy using balance scales to add and take away objects watching the scales move up and down. Try to introduce the words heavier and lighter as they play.

Going outdoors
▲ Take the children to a playground with a see-saw (checking for safety first) and show them how the see-saw moves up and down as heavier and lighter people move on and off.
▲ Hold a long jump contest, measuring the distance jumped in strides and then with a standard ruler.

Weight and volume

Measuring and weighing activities can be great sources of entertainment for children of all ages. Young children simply love filling and emptying games and as children get older they are curious to know how heavy or how full a range of objects are.

What to do

● Pair up some similar-sized objects, such as an apple and a potato, and ask the children to guess, by eye, which is the heaviest. Now let them pick the objects up, one in each hand, and guess by feel. Then check out the objects using the kitchen scales.
● Using some smaller but similar-sized sets of objects, such as dried butter beans, encourage the children to use kitchen scales to find out how many beans weigh the same as one potato.
● Provide a measuring jug filled with water (marked in units of litres and millilitres) and let the children experiment with measuring different quantities into different-sized cups, bowls and containers. Concentrate on the terms empty, full and half empty with younger children.

Length and height

Long before rulers were invented, people had to develop other ways of measuring length, width or height, and one of the most convenient ways of doing this was to use their hands. The height of horses, for example, is still measured in hands.

What to do

● Encourage the children to use their own hands as a unit to measure the length and height of a range of objects as well as themselves! The children can measure themselves by lying flat on the floor on top of a roll of wallpaper and having someone draw round them. They can then use their hands in a side by side movement to work out their own height.

● Show older children how the measurements made with their hands are different to the ones made with yours. Explain that this is why we need standard units such as centimetres. Let your child measure his outline with a ruler.
● Plant a few seeds in plastic cups or trays and leave them to germinate in a warm dark place. Once the seedlings begin to show encourage the children to measure them regularly using observation, non-standard measures such as pencil marks on a wall or more accurately with a ruler.

Distance

With longer lengths and distances, we measure in metres and kilometres, although old-fashioned miles are still the unit of choice. Before these standard units were devised, people had to measure distances by striding them out.

What to do

● Ask the children to stride their longest stride on a piece of card, marking the distance between both feet. They can use their stride measurement to measure the rooms in the house or the garden.
● On short car journeys use the mileometer to measure the distance travelled. Young children will simply love watching the dials move around, older children can be helped to calculate the distance travelled using simple subtraction (by checking the number on the gauge before you leave and then again at the end of the journey).

Top tips

▲ Do not try to complicate the subject with too much mathematics.
▲ Collect a range of yoghurt pots, margarine tubs and other useful containers.
▲ Use measurement examples that the children are familiar with. For example, if your children go swimming they might be familiar with a length of ten or 25 metres (average pool measurements).
▲ Keep a measurement chart in your house so that the children can see their own growth over the course of time.

It's about time!

The concept of the passing of time is one that takes children a long time to learn and fully appreciate. The very beginnings of knowing the time come from knowing the difference between night and day, and anticipating mealtimes and other regular occurrences. There are some fun ways to introduce more standard units of time as you can discover below.

Children of different ages

▲ Create pictorial clocks for toddlers and young children, with pictures of some of their favourite activities dividing up the clock face.

▲ Older children may have their own watches and will enjoy showing off their time-telling skills. Encourage this by asking them to remind you of something at a certain time!

Day and night

Learning to tell the time accurately, using a clock, requires skills that the children may not acquire until well into their school years. However, even very young children can learn something about time, such as why we have night and day.

What to do

● Talk about night and day with the children. Provide some paper and colouring materials and ask them to draw a double-sided picture of a night and day scene. Young children can be helped to draw the moon and stars, and the sun and flowers, for example. Older children may like to draw pictures of themselves at the two different times.

● Make a simple demonstration

using a torch and a globe (or football) to explain in simple terms why we have night and day. Mark the globe with a coloured sticker showing roughly where you and the children are! Ask one of the children to shine the torch on to the globe as you turn it very slowly. When the torch shines on the sticker it is daytime and when the sticker is out of the light it is night-time.

Clocks

Children will learn a lot about what units of time really feel like when they make their own non-standard clocks, such as water and shadow clocks.

What to do

● Make a small hand-held shadow clock by sticking a straw vertically to the edge of a piece of sturdy white card, so that it is at a

right angle to the surface of the card. On a sunny day take the clock outside at 10am and make a chalk mark on the spot where you stand. With the straw at the furthest edge, place the card in full view of the sun. The sun will cast a shadow of the straw, and this can be traced on to the card and marked as 10am. Repeat this at noon and at 2pm, making sure that you stand in exactly the same spot and face in the same direction. Make marks on the card and label each time. At 10am the next day, the children can line up the shadow with the markings on the card to work out the time!

● Make a simple water clock with a plastic bottle with a small hole cut into the bottom and a container to catch the water. Fill the bottle with water and time it as it drips from the hole in the bottom of the bottle. Time the water for one minute. Tip away the remaining water. Block the hole and put the water from the container back into the bottle. Use a marker pen to mark the water line with 'one minute'. Unblock the hole, and the children now have a one-minute water clock!

Just a minute

We are frequently heard telling the children we care for, 'In a minute!'. But what does a minute actually feel like? The children will enjoy the following challenges that will give them an appreciation of just what a minute really is!

What to do

● Use a water clock (see above) or a one-minute egg-timer to time the children as they jump or hop on the spot. How many jumps or hops can they do in one minute?
● Challenge older children to write their name as many times as possible during a one-minute period.
● Find out which getting dressed tasks take more, less or 'about' one minute.
● Use a five-minute timer and challenge the children to a tidy-up session during this time!

Useful equipment
▲ Have a large working model of a standard clock which the children will become familiar with. This could be either a toy clock or a colourful home-made box model. It need not be elaborate, as long as the hands are moveable.
▲ Provide a selection of different types of clocks for the children to explore, include digital, twenty-four hour, alarm and pendulum clocks.
▲ Find a sundial in a park or garden that you can visit.

Children of different ages

▲ Simply enjoy counting rhymes and songs with young children and demonstrate how you use numbers to count out the number of apples to cook and so on.

▲ If you are minding school-age children make the time to ask them about the number work they are doing at school. Perhaps they would like to show you some examples of what they have learned. Look out for any signs of worry and pass the information on to the child's parents.

Count on it!

Children usually learn 1, 2, 3 alongside A, B, C using a variety of books, songs and educational toys. Making counting part of everyday life is a meaningful and interesting way for children to grasp the basics and can be a lot of fun!

Back to basics

The easiest and most obvious way to introduce numbers to small children is through basic counting. Toddlers can generally manage a sequence of numbers up to five or even ten – although at this stage they are simply words. Learning to apply

these numbers to a physical quantity is more tricky and takes lots of practice. The ideas below will give you some starting points.

What to do

● Explore how many eyes, ears, noses and mouths the child has! Let them work out how many you have. This way, the difference between the quantity of one and two soon becomes clear. Do the same with familiar items, such as bricks and crayons.

● Progress to the numbers three and four. How many legs does a dog have? How many buttons on your coat? Make sure that you point to an object at a time as you count. If the child miscounts, stop and start again.

● Count together in useful situations, such as counting out the number of potatoes to peel, or the number of fishfingers to cook.

Sets and groups

Children are naturally good at sorting things! They will sort out the food on the plate that they will eat, the clothes that they will wear and their favourite toys from the toy-box!

What to do

● During tidy-up time ask the children to find all the bricks, or all the pieces of train

Taking it further

▲ Multiplying and dividing are slightly more difficult concepts for young children to grasp. The basic idea of multiplication can be illustrated by asking the children to add together groups of counted objects, such as two lots of apples, bricks or books.

▲ Similarly, dividing is simply sharing out. Take four crayons and ask the child to make sure that you both have an equal number of crayons.

Top tips
▲ Keep number games and activities simple. If the child appears to have had enough and begins to lose concentration, then leave the game for that day.
▲ As with most early skills, the key to success is repetition – using a variety of situations in which counting is both fun and useful.

track to put in the appropriate containers. Without realising it, the children are sorting objects into groups or sets.

● Assemble a collection of items, building blocks of different shapes and colours, or a collection of shoes, for example, and ask the children to sort them by different features. How many round blocks are there? How many red blocks are there? And so on.

One more

Even young toddlers, know the basic meaning of 'more', as they will readily demonstrate when they would like another sweet or push on the swing!

What to do

● Sing traditional songs such as 'Five Hot Cross Buns', 'Five Little Ducks' and 'Ten Green Bottles' to help the children to grasp the concepts of 'one more' and 'one less'. Use your fingers, or actual objects, such as five green plastic bottles, to help the children to visualise the numbers.

● Play with some small cars or other small world toys with the children and ask them to hand you one more for your collection of, say, silver cars. Now count the new amount together, saying 'Two silver cars and one more makes three silver cars!'.

● Go back to your building block collection and ask the child to count out three bricks, laying them in a straight line. Then ask for one more. How many are there in the line now? Very soon the children will get used to the pattern of one and one makes two and so on. Subtraction is the same, only in reverse. Remember to keep the numbers that you are working with fairly low – once you get past ten, the counting can become tedious and more likely to lead to mistakes.

Easy reading

Reading is one of life's most enjoyable pursuits and a vital basic skill. It is not surprising that it is also a subject which can cause anxiety for parents. While reading schemes have changed over the years, along with the arguments about their respective values, one thing remains constant, and that is that children should be encouraged to enjoy books and reading from a very early age.

Children of different ages

▲ Read and share books with babies from the very early days. Your voice and warmth will soothe them and they will soon begin to enjoy the bright colours and shapes found in early picture books.

▲ Provide a set of magnetic letters for your fridge door. Make a new word each day and help older children to read it with you. Vary the complexity of the word to suit the child.

Sharing books

▲ Nothing will develop children's reading skills in a more pleasurable way than simply sitting down to share a good story together! Build up your own mini library from which the children can select their favourites, and swap books with other childminders to keep the selection fresh.

▲ When you read to the children be sure that they can see both the words and the pictures. Move your finger along the words from left to right as you read, to show how the writing works.

▲ Talk about the pictures in the book and encourage the children to offer their own ideas about what happens in the story.

Relax and enjoy

Before learning to read it is of vital importance that children are surrounded by books and print. If they see reading as both fun and a useful part of daily life, they will be more eager to learn how to master it for themselves.

What to do

● Let the children see you reading, whether it is to find out the time of a favourite children's programme, reading a letter or reading the shopping list that you have written yourself.

● Set aside a time for a daily story-reading session. Get all cosy and surround yourselves with books, cushions and favourite cuddly toys. Read old favourites and introduce some new ones.

● Visit the library together. Sit down and help the children to choose their own books. What can they 'read' from the cover? What do they think the story will be about?

Matching pairs

Before children can read, they need the ability to observe in detail. They will be doing this as they share picture books with you, and there are plenty of other games that you can play too…

What to do

● With very young children, begin with games of matching picture pairs – you could use commercially made picture pair games or make your own (see 'Top tips'). Start by arranging the pictures face-up and see if the children can pick out the matching pairs.

● Play picture pairs with older children. This time turn the pictures over and make it a memory game. You may also wish to use pictures with slightly smaller, less obvious detail. They will have to study the pictures a little more closely to identify the pairs, but it is a skill that will be vital when learning to identify letters of the alphabet.

● As a next step, provide matching pictures with letters which represent the picture, for example, a picture of a dog with a letter 'd'. With help the children will begin to recognise some letters and the sounds they make.

Look out for letters

Children love to show off any newly acquired skills and will delight in demonstrating their grasp of letters and letter sounds. Here are some ideas for presenting them with the opportunity!

What to do

● Once the children are able to recognise a few letters, make sure that you look out for them on your walks, or wherever you are. Look at signs, advertisements, shops and buses for any letters that the children can recognise.

● Look out for letters in the home, on boxes, newspapers, notices and so on.

● Bring the idea of letter sounds into your everyday conversation, and make the children aware of their association with items around the house. For example, '"C" is for Carol and carpet and curtains'.

Top tips

▲ Make sure that your approach to early reading and reading is the same as that of the child's parents.

▲ Make your own picture pair cards. Collect duplicates of catalogues and cut out pairs of pictures, the brighter the better, to stick on to small white cards.

▲ Stick to lower-case letters initially, as trying to introduce capitals as well may confuse the children.

▲ Do some fun letter-making activities, such as carving out letters on potatoes cut in half for some potato printing; using lengths of wool to bend and turn into letter shapes; and making letter-shaped biscuits by shaping the biscuit dough before cooking.

Write on!

Learning to write is a process that probably starts long before a child's first formal lessons. There are many ways to encourage pre-writing skills and to develop and maintain a child's enthusiasm for writing. We explore some of them with the ideas below.

Children of different ages

▲ It is generally between the ages of four and six that children begin to form recognisable letters, learning that they are associated with sounds. But preparation for this can begin much earlier, starting with plenty of shared reading and the provision of bright and stimulating lettered images.

▲ Supply older school-age children with plenty of card, paper, sticky tape and staplers, and they will spend hours making their own diaries, gift tags and mini story-books!

Home links

▲ If you are caring for pre-school children, it is important that you discuss the issue of reading and writing with parents and carers. They may be delighted that you can offer support – perhaps they are encouraging their child themselves, in which case you must try to adopt the same approaches, so as not to confuse the child. They may however feel that it is something best left until the start of school, and their wishes must of course be respected.

▲ Keep in touch with the parents or carers and tell them of their child's achievements, however small.

Learning through play

At the early stage of writing, children learn a lot through imitation and through experimenting, often in play situations. Both strategies provide them with the confidence to experiment and 'have a go'.

What to do

● Colourful pictorial 'abc' wall charts provide an opportunity for very young children to learn that 'a' is for apple, 'b' is for ball, and so on, eventually recognising the letter and its accompanying picture.

● Older children will quickly get to grips with alphabet jigsaws and puzzles, making

the sound and shape association as they play. In fact, any activity which involves recognition skills, such as shape sorting toys will be useful.

● Provide plenty of painting and drawing materials for older children to use to copy the words, letters and pictures from your wall chart.

● Encourage the children to become involved in your own writing tasks – helping you to write birthday cards, shopping lists and perhaps making some colourful signs for individual rooms in the house.

Shared reading

Shared reading is a valuable activity, and as recent reports suggest, one of the best ways of introducing children to the concept of written words.

What to do

● Repeat favourite stories frequently. Older children will eventually recognise certain letters and words, and the way they sound, on the page. The next stage is learning to copy them. They will be proud to be able to 'read' the story to you.

● Find some easy-to-read picture books with repetitive phrases. Cover up the words on the page with strips of paper, affixed with Blu-Tack (or use Post-it notes to cover the words). Invite older children to write the words they think will go with the story, either from

memory or their own imaginations. Praise and encourage any attempts. Read back the stories together.

Letter formation

Once a child has reached the stage of learning to write it is very important that they form the letters properly, otherwise, once at school they will have to learn all over again and this will not help their self-confidence.

What to do

● With the parents' permission, and possibly in liaison with the school, invest in one of the commercially available handwriting books. These will include activities to help you guide the children to form their letters in the correct way.

● Help the children to make their own 'abc' wall chart, using words and pictures of their own choice. Cut out an assortment of pictures from magazines and let the children pick out their own picture to correspond with each letter.

● Make personalised name badges, room plaques, book plates and other labels with the children. Invite older children to use decorative script and their best handwriting and encourage early writers to trace over your own writing to form their names. Ensure that they are forming the letters in the correct way.

● Introduce a variety of mediums for drawing and for forming letters. Aside from pencil and paper the children will enjoy diversifying their early writing skills with chalk and board, wax crayons, finger paints, wet sand, Plasticine and play dough.

Resource bank

Story and picture books

- *I Wish I Could Count to a Million* by Joyce Dunbar and Carol Thompson (Hodder) – but look at all the things you can already do!
- *The Stopwatch* by David Lloyd (Walker Books). When Peter gets his stopwatch he can't stop himself from timing how long it takes to do everything!
- *Robert Crowther's Most Amazing Hide and Seek 1 2 3 Numbers Book* by Robert Crowther (Walker Books). One spider drops on its thread, five goldfish leap out of the water, ten butterflies rise in the sky in this wonderful pop-up counting book.

Information/Rhyme books

- *Fun With Sizes* by Peter Patilla and Kirsty Asher (Belitha Press) contains pages of puzzles that require some form of measurement to solve.
- *Counting Rhymes* by Carol Thompson (Orchard Books) will provide hours of musical fun while younger children practice their number skills.
- *One, Two, Buckle My Shoe* (Macmillan). Easy rhymes with numbers for toddlers and young children.
- *One Duck Stuck* by Phyllis Root, illustrated by Jane Chapman (Walker Books). Ten types of animals (from possums to dragonflies) try to get duck unstuck from the mud in this colourful and charming counting rhyme.

Equipment

- An abacus is the oldest calculator known to humans and is still one of the best visual ways for young children to grasp basic number concepts such as addition and subtraction.
- A set of magnetic letters are handy for sticking on the fridge or freezer door to do some simple spelling.

Websites

- www.thebigbus.com
This website hosts a range of online activities involving words and numbers, with tasks specifically aimed at the under- and over-fives.
- www.allparents.co.uk
Lots of early learning online pages packed with interesting ideas for numeracy and literacy activities.

Places to visit

- Find out how time is measured and why it all revolves around the position of the Sun and the stars by spending a day at an astronomy observatory such as **Jodrell Bank Observatory Visitor Centre**, in Macclesfield, near Manchester. Tel: 01477-571 339.
- Look out for Book Festivals and children's reading activities, particularly during the summer holidays, at your local library.
- Bring a favourite fairy tale to life at the **Alice in Wonderland Centre** in Llandudno, North Wales. This imaginative centre contains an indoor walk-through Wonderland Rabbit Hole with life-sized animated displays from the Alice story collection. Tel: 01492-860 082.

CHAPTER 4

Some of the world's greatest chefs began their culinary exploits at a very early age, and there is no reason why children should not learn the basics of cooking and how to find their way around the kitchen while having lots of fun!

Fun with food

Why fun with food?

For some children, mealtimes can become something of a battleground. By encouraging them to be interested and actively involved in what comes out of the kitchen and appears on their plates, it is much easier to tempt them into trying new and different kinds of food. Exploring foods, including dishes from a range of different cultures, helps to broaden the children's tastes, while discovering which foods are the healthiest can help to set sensible eating patterns for life. The following activities are designed to teach children the basics of kitchen safety and hygiene, while allowing them some freedom to explore their own cooking skills. With limited ingredients, the children can be creative, and they will genuinely delight in being able to produce food that looks and tastes delicious.

A range of ages

Age will determine how much the children will be able to manage unaided. Babies and young toddlers love to touch food and most enjoy the sensation of squeezing soft substances, and delight in being allowed to do some mixing with a spoon. Spare a little flour and water for toddlers and let them do some imaginary cooking – varying the consistency to give them a range of sensations! Be prepared for some mess!

Cooker-free recipes remove the risk of danger from a hot stove, and are ideal for toddlers and younger children. Older children will naturally want to progress to more challenging dishes and should be given the opportunity to try new ideas (with careful supervision) – even if they are culinary disasters!

Special advice

The kitchen can be a dangerous place. Safety advice is provided throughout the following chapter, and the importance of safe and hygienic cooking, preparation and clearing away should be emphasised to the children throughout the activities. Always check whether the children suffer from any food allergies, especially nut allergies.

Healthy eating

It is not always easy to persuade children to eat healthily, especially when fast-food alternatives and delicious sweets and biscuits provide a temptation. But by learning about healthy eating from an early age they will find it easier to choose the most sensible foods to eat.

Children of different ages

▲ It is important to get across the message to older children that it is fine to eat 'junk food' occasionally but that a balanced diet of healthy foods is better.
▲ Babies and young children can be notoriously fussy eaters. Make food fun, colourful and varied, and they are more likely to be interested in trying new things.

Food that grows

There is nothing quite so exciting as planting seeds and watching them grow into something that can be eaten. Apart from a sense of achievement at having produced homegrown food, children will also learn a little about the life-cycle of plants.

What to do
● Hard-boil an egg and when cool, let the children paint a face on the shell. Cut off the top, and carefully scoop out the yolk and egg white leaving an empty shell. Dampen some

Questions to ask
▲ Why do we need vitamins to keep healthy and which foods supply them?
▲ Why is too much sugar bad for our teeth?
▲ Can you name three or four foods that are naturally sweet?

cotton wool and push this carefully into the shell and sprinkle mustard cress seeds on top. These will germinate and start to grow within a few days. Once the cress has reached a few centimetres in length, trim it with scissors and mix it with hard-boiled egg to make a delicious sandwich filling.
● If you can spare a tiny corner of your garden, encourage the children to try growing some salad greens.
● Spend an afternoon fruit picking, perhaps wild blackberries or farmed strawberries. Talk about organic food, which does not use chemical pesticides to keep the bugs at bay.

Food for energy

The science behind a balanced diet is a little too complicated for young children, but they can learn about different food groups – what they do, and how a little bit of each can make a balanced healthy meal.

What to do
● Look at the dairy products in your fridge, such as milk, yoghurt and cheese. See if the children know which animal produces them.
● Explain that foods that contain sugar and starch provide us with energy. Tell the children that some foods are healthier energy-givers than others – a banana is better than a bar of chocolate for an instant energy boost. Taste a selection of healthy natural energy-givers together.
● We need some fat to keep our bodies healthy, but too much can cause blockages in the vessels that carry blood around our bodies. Melt a small amount of solid vegetable fat in a bowl in the microwave until

it turns to liquid. (Warn the children not to touch.) Put some on a spoon and see how it sticks to the spoon as it cools.

Sugar and spice

Taste and smell are very important and it is fun to see how good our senses are at detecting them. Let the children try to identify some mystery foods and look together at some of nature's magic when it comes to colour and flavour.

What to do

● Prepare a large plate with a dozen individual samples of food, such as cooked carrot, potato, fruit, cheese and so on. Blindfold the children and let them take turns to see if they can identify the foods by taste.
● Repeat the blindfold test, this time with foods that have a strong smell, for example, mint, lemon, peppers, garlic, cheese and so on. Can the children guess the foods from the smells?
● Find out about other ways of sweetening food, such as putting honey in tea, or adding fruit to cereals instead of sugar.
● Together, think of some different natural foods for each of the colours of the rainbow – red, orange, yellow, green, blue and purple.

The healthy-food test

How much have the children learned about healthy food? Test their knowledge with these fun food quizzes.

What to do

● Prepare a dozen different types of food and ask the children to say whether they are animal or vegetable.
● Name a fruit or vegetable beginning with selected letters of the alphabet or by colour.
● Help the children to sort a bag of shopping into different categories.

Children of different ages

▲ Let older children organise themselves and their equipment and do as much as possible in terms of tidying-up. This helps them to work in an organised and, therefore safer, fashion.
▲ With young children and toddlers the emphasis in the kitchen must be on safety while allowing them to see what is going on.

Getting started

Any activities that involve food need careful preparation and planning. As well as being encouraged to be creative in the kitchen, children need to know the basic rules of hygiene, food storage and the layout of the kitchen.

Preparation

The way to start any cooking activity is by making sure that everything is prepared and ready before you begin – that includes ingredients, utensils and the cook! Equally important is the process that follows food preparation – the clearing-up!

What to do
● Establish a simple getting-ready routine – aprons are fastened, everyone's hands are

washed and the kitchen surfaces are wiped with a clean cloth.
● If you are following a recipe, the children will need to understand the importance of weighing out ingredients on the kitchen scales. You do not need to go into too much detail about metric measure, but even young children will quickly get a sense of proportions and sizes by using the scales.
● Use other measures such as cups and spoons to weigh out ingredients; this will help younger children with counting skills.

At the shops

Children might be forgiven for thinking that everything edible comes from the local supermarket – after all shopping is so much more convenient with everything under one roof. But it is a good idea to venture farther afield now and again to explore the many interesting places that sell food.

Where to go

● Take a walk down your nearest high street and see how many different shops there are that sell food. What are their names and what do they sell?
● In the shops or the supermarket let the children help to choose fresh food such as fruit and vegetables. They can count out the apples, learn how to look for fruits that are ripe, and decide how much food is needed for the number of people involved.
● The fish market is a wonderful place (if a bit smelly) to look at the many varieties of fish that we can eat!
● Visit a local farmer's market where the children can see fresh dairy produce and greengroceries up close. Encourage them to help choose which items are the best to buy.

Get into gear

It is a good idea to look at some of the basic equipment that the children will be using, including kitchen utensils, pots and pans and the cooker itself. Safety should be emphasised at all times.

Safety matters

▲ Keep sharp knives and other implements out of children's reach.
▲ Emphasise the dangers of a hot oven and ensure that children are never left near one unsupervised.
▲ Take extra care if small children have to use a chair or kitchen stool to reach the work surface.
▲ Supervise the washing-up carefully – hot tap water can scald.

What to do

● Lay some basic utensils such as wooden spoons, spatulas and rolling pins on the work surface and invite the children to name them and explain what they are for.
● Show the children some more unusual gadgets, such as egg slicers, pizza cutters and garlic presses and talk about them together.
● You will be using the oven for some of the recipes. Why is the temperature so important? What happens if the oven is too hot or too cool?

Food storage

It is important for children to understand why certain types of food are stored in different ways, and what happens when food is stored in the wrong place. Why are some foods not suitable for freezing? Why must dairy products be kept in the fridge?

What to do

● Buy two or three green, under-ripe bananas. Put one in the fridge and one in the fruit bowl at room temperature. See which one ripens, or turns yellow, first.
● Although freezing is a convenient way of storing a lot of our food, not everything can be kept in the freezer. Try putting some strawberries or blackcurrants in a small sandwich bag and leave them in the freezer for a day to see what happens.
● Dried food, such as pasta, beans and lentils can be stored in the cupboard for several months because they have had all the water taken out of them. Put a few dried beans and lentils in a small bowl, cover with water, and leave for 24 hours. Now they are ready for cooking.

Top tips

▲ Let the children have their own plastic containers with cereals, pulses and other ingredients. Clearly label the containers with labels made by the children themselves.
▲ Use old shirts worn back to front with the sleeves rolled up as aprons to protect the children's clothes.

Cooking without a cooker

There are plenty of tasty dishes that can be prepared without having to turn on a cooker or a microwave, and these make an ideal introduction to food preparation for young children. Without the potential dangers posed by a hot oven or hob, children can experiment with different flavours, colours and textures in safety.

Children of different ages

▲ Older children will want to be a bit more imaginative when it comes to some of the ingredients they use, to find out which flavours work well together and which do not.
▲ Younger children will delight in producing something that looks good, so use ingredients with interesting shapes and colours that can be nicely presented.

Sandwiches

Not only are sandwiches one of the easiest non-cooked meals to prepare; they are also one of the most versatile. There are plenty of ideas for fillings that can be used with different types of bread.

What to do
● 'Super sandwiches' – use biscuit cutters to cut out fun shapes from sandwiches, such as hearts and circles.
● 'Pitta pockets' – slice open a pitta bread to form a pocket, which the children can fill with a mixture of ingredients such as tuna and tomato, or ham and lettuce.
● 'Tortilla treats' – flour tortillas are perfect for wrapping up just about anything. Try cooked chicken, lettuce and soy sauce to make Chinese chicken wraps, or mozzarella cheese, ham and tomato sauce to create pizza wraps.

Special equipment/resources
▲ Electric mixers and blenders take all the hard work out of whipping and blending, but the children should have a try at the same technique using a hand whisk.
▲ For the best results, use well-ripened fruit for the blended drinks.
▲ Where fruit needs to be peeled, let older children use safety peelers.

Salads

There are very few vegetables and fruits that cannot be included in a salad. Crisp, raw, and healthy, they contain all the vitamins and minerals that can be lost when they are cooked – and they taste good too!

Recipes

● *Sweet and crunchy carrot salad*
Ingredients: 500g shredded carrot; 250g raisins; 100g light mayonnaise; 1 tablespoon lemon juice; ½ teaspoon salt; 1 tablespoon brown sugar.
To make: Mix the ingredients in a bowl and serve with slices of crusty bread for a tasty snack.

● *Funny face salad*
Ingredients: A washed leaf from an iceberg lettuce, plus some washed, dried and chopped lettuce; four slices of ham, cut into strips; 50g grated Cheddar cheese; two grapes; one wedge of tomato; a small piece of cucumber.
To make: Place the lettuce leaf in a small serving bowl, sprinkle with grated cheese. Place the grapes and piece of cucumber on the cheese to make the eyes and nose of a face. Cut a wedge of tomato to make a smiley mouth. Add the strips of ham and chopped lettuce to make hair!

Desserts

Most children look forward to dessert, especially when they have made it themselves. The following recipes can be made in advance and kept refrigerated.

Recipes

● *Easy ice-cream*
Ingredients: 100ml cold milk; 1 tablespoon vanilla flavouring; 200g tin of sweetened condensed milk; pinch of salt; 500ml double cream.
To make: Stir the cold milk, vanilla, condensed milk and salt together in a bowl. In a separate larger bowl, whisk the double cream using an electric mixer until it forms firm peaks. Fold the milk mixture into the whipped cream and pour into a shallow tray, cover and freeze for four hours, stirring when the edges start to harden.

● *Fruity jellies*
Ingredients: One packet of jelly; pieces of fruit; water.
To make: Make up a packet of jelly according to the instructions and leave to cool for half an hour. Chop up some fruit and stir into the jelly. Pour into individual dishes or moulds.

Drinks

Healthy fruit drinks and flavoured milkshakes can be enjoyed at any time of the day. Try blending unusual fruits such as pineapple and mango to give a tropical flavour, or citrus fruits such as orange and tangerine for a tangy taste.

Recipes

● *Fruit shakes*
Ingredients: Fruit; vanilla ice-cream.
To make: Choose any type of fruit and equal quantities of vanilla ice-cream. Put into a blender and mix for three minutes until smooth and delicious.

● *Fizzy orange*
Ingredients: 250ml fresh orange juice; 250ml orangeade; 100g dried milk powder; a few ice cubes.
To make: Combine ingredients in blender until smooth and the ice is crushed.

● *Yoghurt shakes*
Ingredients: 200g carton of plain yoghurt; 250ml orange juice; one banana or pear; or a fruit combination.
To make: Combine all the ingredients in a blender until smooth.

Easy snacks

By this stage the children will have tried their hand at making some simple dishes. With careful supervision, they are now ready to do some real cooking – preparing the kind of food that they like to eat.

Children of different ages

▲ Challenge older children to plan a menu with two or three easy courses. You should let them do as much of the preparation and cooking as possible.
▲ Young children will delight in stirring, mixing, and spooning out ingredients.

Fishy dishes

Fish is nutritious, tasty, and can be turned into a wide range of nourishing dishes. Canned or frozen fish is easiest for children to handle as it is ready to use and generally free from bones.

Recipes
● *Fishfinger castle*
Ingredients: Ten fish fingers; instant mashed potato (make up approximately five servings); 200g frozen garden peas.
To make: Grill the fish fingers and boil or microwave the peas, according to instructions. Make up the mashed potato according to the instructions and spoon on to a plate in a square shape. Cut one third off each fish finger and using alternate long and short pieces, stand them upright against the mash to form the castle. Drain the peas and arrange around the base.
● *Toasted tuna melts*
Ingredients: One baguette; 200g can of tuna chunks; 100g grated Cheddar cheese.
To make: Cut the baguette into three or four slices and then cut these in half lengthways. Spoon the tuna chunks on to the baguette pieces, spreading them evenly. Sprinkle the Cheddar cheese on top and grill for five minutes or until the cheese is golden and bubbling.

Safety matters
▲ When handling anything sharp, children should keep the blade or sharp end pointing away from them.
▲ Do not let children reach across the stove for anything and remember that some hobs stay hot long after they are switched off.
▲ Emphasise the importance of keeping uncooked meat away from fresh or cooked foods.
▲ Make sure that children do not handle raw meat and ensure that any adult that does so, washes their hands thoroughly.

Creative play for ages 0 to 8

Chicken dishes

Chicken is a children's favourite – low in fat, extremely versatile, and often best eaten as finger food.

Recipes

● *Fingerlickin' chicken*

Ingredients: 500g boneless chicken breast chopped into bite-sized pieces; one egg; 2 tablespoons milk; 600g crushed Cornflakes.

To make: Preheat the oven to 200°C, or Gas Mark 6. Put the crushed Cornflakes into a large food bag. Whisk together the eggs and milk in a bowl. Dip the chicken pieces in the egg and milk mixture, and then drop, one by one, into the bag of Cornflakes. Fasten the neck of the bag and shake well. Lay the coated chicken pieces on a baking tray and bake for approximately 20 minutes or until done.

● *Cheesy chicken chunks*

Ingredients: 100g chopped, cooked chicken; three hard-boiled eggs, finely chopped; 50g cheddar cheese grated; 3 tablespoons salad cream or Thousand Island dressing; 50g fresh white breadcrumbs mixed with a little chopped parsley for coating.

To make: Mix together all the ingredients, apart from the parsley and breadcrumb mixture. Roll into small balls. Then roll the balls into the breadcrumb mixture and serve.

Cheesy choices

Some supermarkets sell cheese in small individual portions, which allow the children to try some of the more unusual flavours without it costing you a fortune.

Recipes

● *Cheese and ham rolls*

Ingredients: Ten slices of honey roast ham; 100g cream cheese; 2 tablespoons chopped chives.

To make: Spread the cheese on each ham slice, sprinkle with chives, and roll up.

● *Pizza faces*

To make: Buy some plain pizza bases and provide the children with tomato puree, grated cheddar or mozzarella cheese and an assortment of toppings. Include cherry tomatoes, mushrooms, squares of cooked ham and some slices of red, yellow or orange peppers. See who can make the funniest pizza faces using the ingredients!

Veggie snacks

Vegetables often get the thumbs down from children before they have even given them a try. Try to use vegetables with plenty of crunch, taste and colour that children will want to cook and eat.

Recipes

● *Patchwork potatoes*

To make: Bake a large potato for each child (for about one hour). Remove the potatoes from the oven and cut each one in half. Scoop out the insides, place in a bowl and mash with butter and milk. Add some cheese, beans or vegetables, or a combination of these. Place the mixture back in the skins.

● *Edible pepper pot*

To make: Cut a red pepper in half, removing seeds and white pith. Cut one half of the pepper into strips. Wash and chop short sticks of celery, carrot, and cucumber. Place the chopped vegetables in the empty half of the pepper, or veggie bowl, which the children can also eat when it is empty.

CHAPTER

4

Fun with food

Festival foods

Special foods are often prepared to celebrate different holidays and festivals that take place throughout the year. Many of these originate from different countries and cultures and it is fun to look at some of the traditional foods that accompany these festivals.

Children of different ages
▲ Older children will enjoy looking at the meanings behind some of the festivals and the cultures that celebrate them.
▲ Make sure that young children are not given any foods that they may choke on, such as nuts, and chunks of hard fruits.

Chinese New Year (January/February)

'Kung Hey Fat Choy' is the Chinese 'Happy New Year' greeting. New Year is the most important of all Chinese festivals. It is celebrated with a large family meal, and children are presented with lucky money in red envelopes.

Recipe
● *Chinese moon cakes*
Ingredients: 100g sugar; two egg yolks; 100g salted butter; 100g plain flour; 100g strawberry jam.
To make: Preheat the oven to 190°C, or Gas Mark 5. Mix the butter, sugar and one egg yolk in a bowl. Add the flour and continue to mix to form a dough. Roll pieces of the dough into small balls. Make an indent in each ball and fill with half a teaspoon of jam. Brush each moon cake with the other beaten egg yolk and place on a baking tray in the oven for about 20 minutes.

Easter (March/April)

Easter is an important festival of the Christian calendar and is a time for new beginnings. Eggs are a prominent feature of the festival, as they represent new life – but they are most popular in their various chocolate forms!

Recipes
● *Easter nests*
Ingredients: 250g cooking chocolate; 800g cornflakes or puffed rice; chocolate mini eggs to decorate.

To make: Melt the chocolate by breaking it into pieces and placing in a glass bowl over a saucepan of hot water. Mix with the cereal, then spoon the mixture into paper cup cases, moulding each into the shape of a nest. When cool and set, fill with the mini eggs.

Talk about
▲ Why is Divali celebrated with the lighting of lamps and divas?
▲ The Chinese name each year after an animal, such as the Year of the Dog. Ask the children to help you find out which Chinese year they were born in.

● *Easter pancakes*

Ingredients: 100g plain flour; one egg, beaten; 250ml milk; 1 tablespoon vegetable oil; 50g white chocolate, grated.

To make: Add the beaten egg to the plain flour, mixing slowly. Then add the milk and beat to a smooth batter. Heat the oil in a small frying pan and add a little of the pancake batter. When the pancake is cooked underneath, turn it over by tossing and cook the other side. Sprinkle with white chocolate, roll and leave for one minute for the chocolate to melt.

Passover (April)

Passover is a Jewish festival that commemorates the time in history when the Jewish people were freed from slavery in the land of Egypt, and is celebrated at home with family and friends gathering to eat a ceremonial meal.

Recipe

● *Easy matzah balls*

Ingredients: 2 tablespoons vegetable oil; two eggs; 100g matzah meal (available from kosher and speciality delicatessens); 1 teaspoon salt; 1 tablespoon water.

To make: Place together the oil, eggs, matzah meal and salt in a bowl. Mix well, add the water then mix again. Cover with cling film and refrigerate for 30 minutes. Bring a large pan of water to the boil. Take approximately a tablespoon of mixture, roll it into a ball and drop it carefully into the boiling water. Cover and simmer for 40 minutes. The matzah can then be served with chicken or vegetable soup.

Divali (October/November)

Divali is celebrated by both Hindus and Sikhs. It is a festival of lights, symbolising the victory of righteousness and the lifting of spiritual darkness. Lots of sweets and snacks are prepared at this time.

Recipes

● *Kheer*

Ingredients: 1l milk; 200g rice; a few cashew nuts finely chopped; handful of raisins.

To make: Heat the milk and allow to simmer for a few minutes. Add the sugar and stir until it melts. Add the rice, stir, and allow to simmer for 15 minutes (until the rice is cooked). Sprinkle the chopped cashew nuts and the raisins over the top and serve.

● *Coconut barfi*

Ingredients: 200g sugar; water; 200g dried coconut; 50g chopped cashew nuts.

To make: Heat the sugar and water in a pan until it forms thick syrup. Add the coconut and mix thoroughly and then add the chopped cashew nuts. Grease a plate with butter and pour on the coconut mixture, spreading with a knife or spatula. When cool, cut into diamond-shaped pieces with a sharp knife.

Top tips
▲ Make sure that you are aware of any food allergies that the children may have.
▲ Ask anyone that you know of that is celebrating a particular festival to talk to the children and perhaps share some of the special food associated with the festival.

Resource bank

Story and picture books

● *Oliver's Milkshake* by Vivian French and Alison Bartlett (Hodder) is the story of where all the ingredients for a lovely milkshake come from.

● *The Food Fiend* by Liss Norton (Oxford University Press). In this lively story, we learn about a baby who eats everything, except food that is good for it! How can mummy and daddy get baby to eat the right food?

Information books

● *Children's Cookbook* (Usborne). Characters from the *Farmyard Tales* series show how to make and cook a range of simple biscuits, cakes and other treats. Advice on how the finished items can be wrapped and given as gifts is included.

● *The Lunch Bunch* by Gina Steer (Quintet Publishing) provides recipes for young children with easy-to-follow instructions that produce delightful ideas for a tasty lunch.

● Annabel Karmel's *New Complete Baby and Toddler Meal Planner* (Ebury Press) provides a wealth of tasty meal and treat ideas and a reassuring meal planner.

Equipment

● Make cake-mix piping bags by cutting a circle of greaseproof paper, folding it into quarters and snipping a tiny hole off the end.

● Make slushy drinks, ice-lollies, fruit drinks and colourful ice-cube shapes using a Mr Frosty ice-lolly-making and drink-making set. Available from Argos and other high-street toy retailers.

Website

● www.botham.co.uk
Fun, simple recipes, clearly indicating those which the children can manage alone and those which need more adult supervision. Easy to navigate and understand.

Places to visit

● Children will love a visit to **Cadbury World** in Birmingham, West Midlands, which includes a tour of the chocolate factory, demonstrations and opportunities for tasting. For more information call 0121-451 4180 or visit www.cadburyworld.co.uk

● Take a stroll around **a farmers' market** where farmers, growers or producers from a local area sell their own produce direct to the public. This is an opportunity to take a look at fascinating products that have been grown, reared, caught, brewed, pickled, baked, smoked or processed by the stallholder. For a list of events call the National Association of Farmers' Markets. Tel: 01225-787 914.
www.farmersmarkets.net

CHAPTER 5

Games to play

All children love to play games, whether it is alone, in pairs, or in larger groups. Although a lot will depend on their ages and social skills, the following chapter contains plenty of ideas for games that will appeal to everyone.

Why games to play?

Playing games should be more than just a way of passing a couple of hours when there is nothing else to do. Structured games with rules and boundaries instil a sense of fair play, taking turns, and sharing. It is fine to encourage good-natured competition – children like to achieve and feel successful, but this must be tempered with the art of being a good sport and sharing the pleasure of success with competitors.

Team games often depend on good communication – another skill that will be valuable throughout life. Most importantly, playing games is one of the best ways for children to build social skills and boost their self-confidence, as well as being a thoroughly enjoyable way of feeling that they belong to a group.

A range of ages

Games should be challenging and fun for children. It may take a while for young children to understand the concept of taking turns, but by playing in a group they learn the rules more readily. Older children will be able to devise variations on many of the games in this chapter, which should be encouraged. But they must also be patient where younger children are involved in the games and learn to show by example.

Special advice

Many of the games in this chapter are designed to see who is the fastest, most accurate, best catcher and so on – but this is intended in a very lighthearted fashion. Do not let competitive spirit overshadow the fun. Praise the winner but reward everybody for taking part.

Ball games

Ball games are excellent for encouraging team play and for developing hand–eye co-ordination. There are endless variations on the theme of ball games, and although they are generally outdoor activities, some of the gentler ones can be done indoors, if there is room.

Children of different ages

▲ Choose balls that are not too hard, as older children do not always know their own strength when throwing them around the house or near windows.

▲ Babies enjoy hitting balls that are suspended over them, such as on mobiles or playmats. Crawling babies love to pursue soft and textured balls around a room. Use fairly large balls for toddlers so that they can easily grip them with two hands.

Catch it!

One of life's frustrations as a child, is learning to catch a ball, and some people are naturally better at it than others. But as with many new skills, practice may not make perfect – but it helps!

What to do

● Stand the children in a circle and give each child a number. The first child will call out a number and throw the ball to the respective child, who must catch it and then call out a different number and so on. To adapt this game for younger children, simply call out the children's names and either roll or gently pass the ball to each other.

● Collect some different-sized balls. Which is the easiest to catch five times in a row?

● Challenge the children to catch the ball with left hand or right hand only.

● Encourage two older children to throw and catch two balls between them simultaneously. This requires very good co-ordination but practice will bring rapid improvements.

Safety matters

▲ Very small rubber balls that bounce hard and fast need to be used under close supervision, as they can cause damage or injury.

▲ Although some of the activities require a fairly hard surface to bounce the balls on, choose a grassy area, where possible, in order to provide a safer landing surface if there are any mishaps.

▲ Avoid throwing and catching games in any area where there are windows or other property that could be damaged.

Throw it

Whether or not the children go on to become keen cricketers or netball stars, being able to throw a ball accurately and with the right amount of strength is a useful skill for them to have.

Aim to provide a range of fun activities with different sizes and types of balls to encourage the children's developing skills.

What to do

● Balance a bucket at an angle, using bricks or cushions so that it tilts at 45 degrees, with the 'mouth' pointing towards the children. Challenge them to throw a tennis ball into the bucket, getting it to stay in!

● Set up a row of targets, such as small beanbags or empty plastic bottles, on a raised surface (such as a table or a wall). Provide a very soft ball and encourage the children to try and knock the targets off.

● Try throwing overarm and underarm. Which is more accurate?

● See how accurate the children's throws are when they cannot see the target! Place an empty plastic bucket behind the children. Let them see where it is before turning around and throwing the ball over their heads to try and hit it!

Top tips

▲ Some children are better at ball games than others, so praise success at ball skills and make light of mishaps.

▲ To help children that are having difficulties handling balls, first try out some throwing and catching games using soft objects such as beanbags.

Roll it

Rolling is a much gentler activity, but requires just as much skill and judgement as the rest!

What to do

● Set up a mini obstacle course using large books for ramps or tunnels, and see if the children can roll their ball around the course.

● Use an upturned fastened umbrella to play a fun version of croquet, where the children must use the umbrella to try and knock the ball around the course.

● Line up a set of plastic bottle skittles, spaced far enough apart to require some skill to roll the ball and knock more than one down at a time.

Bounce it!

Some balls are bouncier than others! Some are made of solid rubber and these bounce incredibly high, whereas other lighter, plastic balls hardly bounce at all. Use a variety of balls to try the activities below.

What to do

● Show toddlers what is meant by the word bounce. Let them drop a ball down some steps to watch it bounce.

● See how many times you can bounce a ball. Challenge the children to find out if it's easier to use one or both hands.

● Stand facing a large wall. Throw a ball against the wall and as it lands and bounces, try to leapfrog over it!

● Use a piece of coloured chalk to colour an old tennis ball. Throw the ball against a wall to make chalk patterns where it lands. Draw a chalk circle or target and ask the children to aim for the centre of it. The chalk mark left by the ball will reveal who is closest.

Children of different ages

▲ Games for groups of older children will be more sophisticated and competed for rather more fiercely. Do not put too much emphasis on winning and losing.
▲ Younger children may find it more difficult to understand the concept of taking turns, so be patient!

■●▲■●▲■●▲■●▲■●▲■●▲■●▲■

Games for groups

Taking part in larger group activities gives children a sense of belonging and makes them feel valued as a member of a team. Group games can be an effective way of building relationships, and helping children to understand that winning is not everything.

Team games

There are lots of games and activities that children can do in teams – in many ways, the more members of each team the better. Make some team colours, badges or sashes to identify each team.

Safety matters

▲ Ensure that there are no sharp corners or dangerous obstacles during the blindfold games. Be ready to step in and lend a guiding hand.
▲ Do not let group games get out of hand, especially when little ones are taking part.

What to do

● Have relay races between teams of three to four children and ask the children to shout encouragement to their team members.
● A 'Tug of war' is a test of strength in numbers – but only if everyone pulls at the same time. Try to balance the teams evenly by age and size, and then see what happens when you make one team bigger or older than the other.
● A game of 'Pass the balloon' requires the members of each team to pass a balloon backwards, alternately, over their head and under their legs, to the person behind. The last member of the team runs to the front

and starts the process again. Continue until the first team member is back at the front of the line.

Test your skills

Running in a relay race is fine for fast runners! Try a few different kinds of races and contests and discover if the fastest runners make the fastest hoppers or whether it comes down to different skills and abilities.

What to do

● Set challenges for younger children to run, skip or roll to a specified target.
● Hold hopping races, using left foot only, and then right foot only. To make it slightly more difficult, ask the children to alternate feet every five hops.
● Skipping with a rope is a tricky skill for children to learn. The best way to start is by turning the rope as they run so that they are effectively jumping over the rope each time it hits the floor.
● Have a long jump challenge. Lay two markers (rulers or strips of plastic) a short distance apart and ask the children to try and jump over them without touching them. Slowly increase the gap between the markers and see how far the children can jump.

Circle games

Playing games in a circle gives children the opportunity to watch what the others are doing while they do the activity, too. This form of play is very useful at helping children overcome shyness or self-consciousness while having tremendous fun.

What to do

Gather the children into a wide circle around one child who is chosen to be the lookout. The object is to move towards the child in the centre without being seen. The lookout must close their eyes for periods of anything between two and five seconds (let them count under their breath) and then open

their eyes to see if they can spot anyone moving. The game is over when someone manages to reach and touch the lookout without having been spotted!
● Put some music on and ask the children to dance energetically. When the music stops they must freeze like statues in whichever position they are in, not moving until the music comes back on.

Blindfold games

These activities will help children to develop their communication skills when giving directions or instructions, and their listening skills when they have to follow them.

What to do

● Set up a mini obstacle course (such as two rows of chairs that form a corridor, or boxes on the floor that have to be avoided). One child is blindfolded and must get to the other side of the room by following the instructions of another child who guides her around the obstacles.
● Play a variation on 'Blind man's buff', where a blindfolded child has to identify his or her friends by feel alone.

Top tips
▲ If you are going to award prizes for a contest, make sure that everyone gets something. Emphasise it is not the winning, but the taking part that counts.
▲ Make some medals by covering cardboard discs in foil and attaching them to ribbons. The children will love them!

Children of different ages
▲ Older children are more likely to improvise on some of the games and activities and this should be encouraged.
▲ Young children with shorter attention spans will probably enjoy potted versions of some of the games.

Rainy-day games

You do not need to let bad weather spoil your fun! There are plenty of games and activities that the children can do to pass the time on a wet afternoon. They will enjoy them so much, it is unlikely that they will even notice the rain!

Memory games

Children are generally very good at remembering things and these games will test their memory skills, as well as helping them to boost their memory power.

What to do
● Place a dozen small household objects, such as a comb, an apple and a paper clip, on a tray. Give the children one minute to study the objects, then cover the tray with a tea towel and see how many they can recall.
● Cut out 20 small squares of white card. Make ten matching pairs by drawing symbols

such as hearts, stars and so on, on to pairs of cards. Mix them up, place them face-down, and then take turns to see who can match the most pairs.
● Choose a theme such as 'Places', 'Names' or 'Animals' and decide on an opening line, such as 'I went to the zoo and saw…', at which point the first child must think up an appropriate name or object beginning with the letter 'a', for example, 'apple'. Continue through the alphabet, remembering all the previous items.
● Encourage toddlers to remember and talk about two or three things that they did yesterday.

Going outdoors
▲ Once the rain clears, and the ground is dry, take a blanket outside and play some of the games outdoors.
▲ Have an outdoor treasure hunt with a chalk arrow trail to follow.
▲ Invite the children to sit and try some outdoor sketching or painting.

Drawing games

These activities are not so much a test of drawing ability but a means of developing co-ordination and communication skills. Some of the results will be hilarious.

What to do

● Sit two children on the floor, back to back, and give each a drawing pad and a pencil. One is the leader – the other, the follower. The leader begins to draw, describing out loud what they are drawing to the follower, who must try to interpret these instructions on paper. Are the two drawings alike?

● Rest a piece of paper on a book and ask the child to place this on top of his head. Ask him to draw a picture, such as a boat on a lake, or a car on a road, while the paper is on top of his head!

● Give each child a sheet of paper. Ask them to secretly draw just the head of an animal on the paper, which they then fold over so that just the neck is visible. Each child passes their paper to the person on their right and then draws the body of their animal on the new sheet of paper. Do the same with the legs. Unfold the papers and give names to the jumbled animals.

● Start a snake or a circle for a toddler to continue. Alternatively, draw a half-finished vehicle and ask the child to add, for example, the wheels or the windows.

Mystery games

Children love solving puzzles and mysteries by following clues. The following activities will encourage them to get thinking.

What to do

● Choose an object or a famous person, and give the children 20 questions to try and guess who or what you are.

● Send the children out of the room and hide a small object. Then let the children come and find it, with the clues 'warmer' if they are getting close, or 'colder' if they are moving away.

● Have a treasure hunt. Hide the treasure somewhere in the house. Write four or five clues on pieces of card that they must solve in turn to find the next clue, and so on, until they reach the treasure.

Homemade games

Traditional games such as *Snakes and Ladders* and *Ludo* are perennial favourites with children. With a little creative effort they could make their own variations on these popular board games.

What to do

● Make an alternative dice. Draw a hexagonal shape on card; mark out six segments and number it 1–6. Cut out the card and push a blunt pencil through the centre.

● Using a large sheet of sturdy card, draw out a basic route with numbered squares and a 'Start' and a 'Finish'. Add a theme such as 'Race to the beach'. Use the home-made spinner and buttons for counters, to see who wins the game.

● Make a set of dominoes using pieces of card. Instead of dots, decorate them with different colours and patterns.

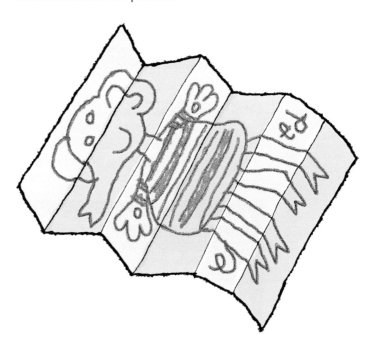

Children of different ages
▲ Games that involve gathering and recording information will appeal to older children and they can make some elaborate charts to log their findings.
▲ Younger children's attention may not stretch to waiting for a particular vehicle to appear. Use games that involve simple colours or guessing games involving vehicles that are in plentiful supply on the roads.

Car games

Anyone who has been on a long car journey with small children will know how difficult it can be to keep them occupied and amused. Keeping their minds active is one way of passing the time, and they will be surprised how much there is to see when they are really looking.

Are we nearly there?

Looking out for certain items will, temporarily, keep children's minds off the length of a journey and how far there is still to go.

Asking questions
▲ How many wheels do different vehicles have?
▲ What is the speed limit on the different types of road?
▲ What does the letter 'L' on drivers' 'L' plates stand for?

What to do
● Look at the different road signs and see if the children can work out what they mean. Look, for example, at signs with numbers, and signs with animals and encourage the children to guess what they show.
● Count how many bus stops the car passes within a set time, such as one or three minutes.
● With older children, watch the car's mileage gauge and see if it increases at the same rate as the road distance signs indicate. For example, if the sign says one mile to Services, or a particular destination, see if the car's clock shows the same.

Colour and counting

You can see cars of almost every colour on the roads nowadays, and unless the children are older and particularly knowledgeable on makes and models of cars, colour is the best way to identify different types of cars.

What to do

● Make a score chart for each child and give them a pen. They must look out for different coloured cars and score one point for red, two for blue and so on. This will obviously work better on quieter roads, as their mental arithmetic may not keep up with the volume of traffic on a motorway!
● Make another chart, this time to list different types of vehicles, such as buses, trucks, motorcycles and so on.
● Draw a grid on a sheet of paper and give the children colouring pencils. Every time they see a car, they must shade in one square using the right colour.
● Have a competition to see who can spot the first double-decker bus, caravan or bike.

On the motorway

Motorway trips are usually the lengthiest and, unfortunately, often offer the least in terms of passenger views. But if you know what to look out for then there is plenty of action on the motorway itself, as the children will discover with the following ideas.

What to do

● Look at the names on the side of passing trucks and lorries and try to find one for each letter of the alphabet.
● Make a very basic copy of the map route you are taking, marking major landmarks and junctions. Encourage the children to follow the route and add any new landmarks that they see to their map.
● Decide on a 'big five' together and look out for the vehicles, such as a lorry, transporter, coach, jeep and caravan. When the children have spotted them all, provide a treat, such as a slice of apple or a new book!

Singalong

Singing as you go is one way of passing time when there is not very much for the children to see outside. Choose songs that the children will have to really think about to encourage them to focus on something other than how much further there is to travel!

What to do

● Teach the children some of the old classic counting songs, such as 'One Man Went To Mow', which involves counting on, and 'Ten Green Bottles', which requires counting back in ones.
● Choose some of the children's favourite pop songs or nursery rhymes and periodically stop, allowing them to fill in the missing lines. Perhaps they can think up alternative lines that rhyme.
● Older children might want to try singing 'a round' with songs such as 'London's Burning'. The first child sings the first line and as they begin the second line, someone else begins the first line. It is tricky, but done properly, sounds delightful!
● Play 'Name that tune' – think of a well-known song, hum the first few notes and see how quickly the children can guess the name of the song.

Top tips
▲ Give little prizes for being able to count cars or chart colours, but be wary of giving too many edible goodies as this can lead to tummy upsets on a long journey.
▲ Keep scrap paper, puzzle books, pencils and something to rest the paper on, in a special travel bag that can be kept permanently in the car.

CHAPTER
5
Games to play

Children of different ages

▲ Let older children think of variations of the activities that you have planned. Encourage them to be experimental with water and shadow play.
▲ Remember that younger children will tire easily, so allow some rest in between games.

Outdoor fun

Fresh air and plenty of space are ideal ingredients for a day of outdoor activities. The garden will be fine as long as you don't have too many flowers and plants that could be spoiled. Weather permitting; a picnic down at the local park is the perfect way to kick off your outdoor fun.

Safety matters

▲ Beware of bumps if the children are racing or jumping about on a hard surface.
▲ If you do go to the park check carefully for hazards such as broken glass before you begin any activities.
▲ If you are away from home, keep an ongoing head count of the children. Arrange for extra adult help to be available when taking younger children away from home. And do not forget to get parental permission for any outings!

Water games

Water play is guaranteed to keep children happy. They are fascinated by water and there are lots of opportunities to encourage children to experiment with it while having plenty of fun.

What to do

● Set up a row of targets on a wall, for example, empty plastic bottles, cans or skittles. Then see who among the children has the best aim with water squirted from a squeezy bottle!

■▲●■▲●■▲●■▲●■▲●■▲●■▲●■▲●■▲●■

● Fill buckets or bowls with water – one for each child, and place an empty bucket or bowl at the opposite end of the garden. Using a plastic cup, let the children have a race to see who can transfer the water from the full bucket to the empty bucket – and see who spills the most!

● Fill a large pan or casserole dish with water. Find as many small items as you can and experiment to discover which ones float and which ones sink.

Sports day

If you can gather enough children together, why not hold your own mini Olympics? But forget the 100-metre hurdles and hammer throwing – this is sports competition with a difference!

What to do

● 'Welly wanging' – place the Wellington boot at the end of the child's foot so that it hangs quite loose and then see who can kick or 'wang' their boot the furthest.

● 'Egg and spoon race' – hard-boil some eggs, one per contestant, and place each on a spoon. If you have children of different ages, give the older ones a flatter wooden spoon to make the race a little fairer!

● Gather some vegetable sacks – your local greengrocer will probably be able to oblige – and hold a sack race to see who can jump their way to the finishing line.

● A three-legged race requires a bit more concentration and co-operation, and would be more suitable for pairs of older children. Tie the right leg of one child to the left leg of the second using a scarf or tie (something quite soft) and see if they can walk without falling over.

Shadows

You will need a fairly bright sunny day for these activities. Ideally choose early morning or late afternoon to get the biggest shadows. If it does become overcast, a powerful torch can be used to boost your light source.

What to do

● Look at shadows formed by trees and plants and other objects in the garden at different times of the day. Why do the shadows change shape?

● While one child stands perfectly still and casts a shadow on the wall or ground, let another child draw around the outline of the shadow with chalk.

● Make a shadow clock. Push a length of wood three feet in length into the soil. At nine o'clock in the morning, go out and mark the top of the stick's shadow with a stone or pebble. Repeat at midday and three o'clock, or more frequently if you want to have more times on the clock.

Chalk it up

Outdoor drawing with chalk gives children the freedom to express themselves without worrying about causing damage or leaving a mess. The rain, or a quick rinse with the hosepipe, will wash it away.

What to do

● Use coloured chalk to mark out a hopscotch grid. Throw a pebble into one of the numbered squares and the children must alternately hop and skip to the square, retrieve the stone and hop/skip back.

● Chalk some stepping stones on to the ground that the children must step on without touching the ground around them.

■▲●■▲●■▲●■▲●■▲●■▲●■▲●■▲●■▲●■

Creative play for ages 0 to 8

Resource bank

Story and picture books
● *Brer Rabbit the Great Tug-O-War* by John Agard and Korky Paul (Red Fox). A Brer Rabbit story in which the wily rabbit outsmarts the heavier opposition team in a tug-o-war contest.
● *What Shall we Play?* by Sue Heap (Walker Books). Matt wants to play trees, Martha wants to play cars and Lily May wants to play fairies but who will get their wish?

Information books
● *Pop-Up Toddlerobics* by Zita Newcombe (Walker Books) provides ten favourite nursery rhymes complete with all the actions.
● *Oranges and Lemons* by Ian Beck and Karen King (Oxford University Press) has plenty of music and movement games inspired by popular children's songs.

Equipment
● Search out an old-fashioned marble set and play, in miniature, some of the rolling games suggested in this chapter.
● Make a personalised set of skittles using a dozen empty plastic pop bottles, half-filled with sand and painted different colours.
● Buy a *Hopscotch and Other Games* kit from Parragon, complete with rulebook and a set of chalks. Available from most retailers and supermarkets.

Websites
● www.kidsdomain.com
Online games and brainteasers centred around a host of themes, including animals, science, space and dinosaurs.
● www.kids-channel.co.uk
Online games and activities for all ages, many based on good hand eye co-ordination and very basic computer mouse and keyboard skills.

Places to visit
● Make the most of an opportunity for play in a wonderful setting such as **Kingsbury Water Park** in north Warwickshire. With over 600 acres of country park, water sports, nature trails, fishing and two adventure playgrounds, it is a real play away. Tel: 01827-872 660.
● Go to watch your local football, rugby or cricket team play a match or arrange to support older siblings at a school match.
● Visit your nearest **Museum of Childhood** to find out about some of the games that grandparents played when they were children.

Further information

Training and qualifications

There are plenty of opportunities for creative playwork, either as a childminder in your own home, or as a playworker in a nursery, pre-school or playgroup. Alternatively you could get involved in one of the many Playwork schemes such as out-of-school clubs and holiday play schemes. These offer childcare before and after school and all day long during the school holidays, and include a wide range of activities, such as sports, drama, arts and crafts, and music, aimed at children aged between 4 and 14.

There are several qualifications relevant to childcare and playwork and many of these are available from local colleges, either on a full-time, part-time basis, or day release for those already in full time employment. Qualifications such as National Vocational Qualifications (NVQs) are flexible and can be studied at your own pace. Financial help for training may be available from College Access funds – contact your local college or your Early Years Development and Childcare Partnership (see below) for details of courses in your area.

The most popular qualification taken by childminders is a Certificate in Childminding Practice (a vocational qualification at Level 3, run by CACHE, the Council for Awards in Children's Care and Education, in association with the National Childminding Association).

For playwork there are a number of short introductory courses, such as CACHE Level 2 Certificate in Playwork, that will give you the basic skills needed to work in an out-of-school setting. You could then complete a NVQ Level 2 qualification to become an Assistant Playworker, or progress towards a supervisory role by gaining a NVQ Level 3 qualification.

Useful contacts

● Department for Education and Skills (DfES) – Early Years Development Childcare Partnerships. Website: www.dfes.gov.uk/eydcp/

● Early Years National Training Organisation (EYNTO). Website: www.early-years-nto.org.uk, tel: 01727-738 300.

● Council for Awards in Children's Care and Education (CACHE). Website www.cache.org.uk, tel: 01727-847 636.

● National Childminding Association (NCMA). Website: www.ncma.org.uk, tel: 020-8464 6164.

● National Centre for Playwork Education – NE works in partnership with agencies in the north east of England to develop, support and promote access to a variety of qualification routes for playworkers who work with school age children. Tel: 0191-215 6279/6208.

● The Pre-School Learning Alliance – a national charity that supports the early education and development of children through community-based groups. Website: www.pre-school.org.uk, tel: 020-7833 0991.

● Playtrain – a creative alternative to traditional playwork. Website: www.playtrn.demon.co.uk, tel: 0121-766 8446.

● National Early Years Network. Website: www.neyn.org.uk, tel: 020-7607 9573.

● www.childcarestudy.org.uk is a new online study service that offers students the freedom to study at their own pace and in their own time. For further details, visit the website or tel: 0116-239 4779. National

Further information

Extension College (NEC) does this, too (see their website: www.nec.ac.uk, tel: 01223-400 200).

Further reading
● *Nursery Education* (Scholastic) is a monthly magazine packed full of theme-based activity ideas, and all the latest early years news and information plus full-colour educational posters. Available on subscription, contact Scholastic, tel: 01926-816250 or visit the website: www.scholastic.co.uk
● *Curriculum Guidance for the Foundation Stage* (QCA). The official handbook containing the early years foundation stage curriculum complete with Stepping Stones and Early Learning Goals for all six Areas of Learning. Website: www.qca.org.uk, tel: 01787-884 444.
● *Play and Learning for the Under 3's* by Jennie Lindon, Kevin Kelman and Alice Sharp (TSL Education Ltd)
● *Child Development and Learning 2–5 Years* by Cath Arnold (Hodder)
● *Learn Through Play; Babies, Toddlers and the Foundation Stage* by Tina Bruce (Hodder Headline).

Activity, rhyme and song books
● Scholastic (www.scholastic.co.uk) publish a range of activity books and series for carers and practitioners of early years children. Of particular interest are the series *Activity Chest*, with titles such as *10-minute Games*; *Regular Routines* and *Multicultural Activities*, and *100 Learning Games*, with titles for the under-threes and the three- to five-year-old age ranges, such as *100 Language Games*.
● *Practical Guide to Activities for Young Children* by Christine Hobart and Jill Frankel (Stanley Thornes)
● *This Little Puffin...* compiled by Elizabeth Matterson (Puffin Books), which is an invaluable book containing songs, rhymes and games for every occasion
● *Okki-Tokki-Unga* (A & C Black), containing 55 all-time favourite action songs.

Special needs
If you are caring for children with special educational needs it is important to include them in as many activities as possible. Many of the activities in this book can be adapted so that everyone can take part, but what is needed is careful forward planning. It is important to be aware of disabilities, and to make other children aware of them too. You must consider all the risk factors, but at the same time, encourage children's confidence in the activities they are able to take part in. Plan outings or activities carefully, and find out whether you will need any specialist equipment.

Your local authority Early Years Development Childcare Partnership can provide further advice on local facilities and resources, for example, special needs toy libraries, loan services and funding for support groups.

Scholastic also publish a series entitled *Special Needs in the Early Years*, which is a series of books to help you to recognise and understand a wide range of special needs and conditions. Titles include *Speech and Language Difficulties*, *Behavioural and Emotional Difficulties* and *Medical Difficulties*, all by Dr Hannah Mortimer. See the Scholastic website on www.scholastic.co.uk for more information.